T0290743

# Spaces that Tell Stories

# AMERICAN ASSOCIATION
# FOR STATE AND LOCAL HISTORY
# BOOK SERIES

## ABOUT THE SERIES

The American Association for State and Local History Book Series addresses issues critical to the field of state and local history through interpretive, intellectual, scholarly, and educational texts. To submit a proposal or manuscript to the series, please request proposal guidelines from AASLH headquarters: AASLH Editorial Board, 2021 21st Ave. South, Suite 320, Nashville, Tennessee 37212. Telephone: (615) 320-3203. Website: www.aaslh.org.

## ABOUT THE ORGANIZATION

The American Association for State and Local History (AASLH) is a national history membership association headquartered in Nashville, Tennessee, that provides leadership and support for its members who preserve and interpret state and local history in order to make the past more meaningful to all people. AASLH members are leaders in preserving, researching, and interpreting traces of the American past to connect the people, thoughts, and events of yesterday with the creative memories and abiding concerns of people, communities, and our nation today. In addition to sponsorship of this book series, AASLH publishes *History News* magazine, a newsletter, technical leaflets and reports, and other materials; confers prizes and awards in recognition of outstanding achievement in the field; supports a broad education program and other activities designed to help members work more effectively; and advocates on behalf of the discipline of history. To join AASLH, go to www.aaslh.org or contact Membership Services, AASLH, 2021 21st Ave. South, Suite 320, Nashville, Tennessee 37212.

# Spaces that Tell Stories

## Recreating Historical Environments

Donna R. Braden

ROWMAN & LITTLEFIELD
*Lanham • Boulder • New York • London*

Published by Rowman & Littlefield
An imprint of The Rowman & Littlefield Publishing Group, Inc.
4501 Forbes Boulevard, Suite 200, Lanham, Maryland 20706
www.rowman.com

6 Tinworth Street, London SE11 5AL, United Kingdom

British Library Cataloguing in Publication Information Available

**Library of Congress Cataloging-in-Publication Data**

Names: Braden, Donna R., author.
Title: Spaces that tell stories : recreating historical environments / Donna
    R. Braden.
Description: Lanham : Rowman & Littlefield, [2019] | Series: American
    Association for State And Local History book series | Includes
    bibliographical references and index.
Identifiers: LCCN 2019014029 (print) | LCCN 2019018950 (ebook) | ISBN
    9781538111048 (Electronic) | ISBN 9781538111024 (cloth : alk. paper) |
    ISBN 9781538111031 (pbk. : alk. paper) | ISBN 9781538111048 (electronic :
    alk. paper)
Subjects: LCSH: Historical museums—Exhibitions—Planning. | Historical
    museums—United States. | Historic sites—Conservation and
    restoration—United States. | Interpretation of cultural and natural
    resources—United States. | Museums—Curatorship—United States.
Classification: LCC AM151 (ebook) | LCC AM151 .B723 2019 (print) | DDC
    907.4—dc23
LC record available at https://lccn.loc.gov/2019014029

# Contents

# List of Illustrations

## FIGURES

## TABLES

# Foreword

When Donna Braden asked me to provide a brief foreword to this book, I was both pleased and honored—pleased because creating immersive and authentic environments in exhibits and historic houses has been at the center of my own museum career for over four decades and honored because Donna is a highly respected colleague I have known during most of that time.

Currently the senior curator and curator of public life at The Henry Ford, Donna has spent over forty years at that museum, which has been a leader in best practices covering so many aspects of public history. Her strong background as a curator and experience developer provides a deep reservoir of proven competence as well as a perceptive lens for tackling the topic of creating historic environments and immersive experiences for history museumgoers.

In this book, museum professionals at historic museums, sites, and houses will get a comprehensive look at the reasons why it's worth—*still* worth, I would say—creating and using period environments to interpret history in our various settings to provide our visitors with incredible and memorable experiences. From planning considerations and research methodology, to story development, to exhibit implementation and visitor evaluation, Donna has comprehensively covered a large universe. The case studies are recent and of much value.

Her goal is to help us all get closer to perfection in immersing people in the past. I say "closer to perfection" because we know that real-time travel is always an elusive goal. But, like many things in life, even near perfection is definitely worth striving for, and I think the readers will find in this book great blueprints to adapt to create their own success stories.

John A. Herbst
Former President and CEO
Indiana Historical Society

# Preface

Historical environments delight visitors by making them feel transported to another time and place. These environments, found in both museum exhibitions and historic structures, are usually rich with objects that hint at deeper stories and context. But these spaces often lack rigor in terms of historical and interpretive methodology along with a thoughtful and purposeful integration of storytelling principles. *Spaces That Tell Stories: Recreating Historical Environments* provides a road map for applying this rigor and integrating these principles into the creation of such environments.

## DEFINING HISTORICAL ENVIRONMENTS

For the purpose of this book, I am defining historical environments as richly detailed environments that evoke the lives and activities of people in the past. They generally:

- Involve a physical setting or space, not a space purely simulated through media or virtual reality.
- Can be of any size, great or small.
- Are situated within the context of human habitation, usually a specific time and place. Though the actual past can never really be known and these environments can never truly recreate the past, rigorous historic research ensures the best accuracy. Although there is much we can learn from natural history dioramas that represent purely natural environments or animals within natural environments, this book does not include them. Natural materials can certainly, however, be incorporated into historical environments.

- Contain a purposeful assemblage of artifacts (and/or replicas of artifacts or other reasonable substitutions) that represent human activity, meant to reinforce the context and the story. In the absence of artifacts, this can also be accomplished through suggestions of artifacts through, for example, lighting, shadows, and sound.
- Tell a compelling story through the use of one or more interpretive techniques. Ideally, this story ignites the imagination through drama, narrative, multisensory components, and a good understanding of target audience(s).
- Align with and reinforce the museum's mission and vision as well as the Big Idea of the exhibition (described in chapter 3) or the interpretive plan of the historic structure or site. This distinguishes them from environments that exist for commercial, for-profit purposes.

## HOW I CAME TO WRITE *SPACES THAT TELL STORIES: RECREATING HISTORICAL ENVIRONMENTS*

I'm sure I'm not alone in admitting that I was drawn to historical environments in museums at a young age. My earliest memory of feeling mystically transported back in time by one of these was in elementary school, when my third-grade class visited the Pioneer Log Cabin at the Western Reserve Historical Society in Cleveland, Ohio, where I grew up. The postcard that I purchased that day as a souvenir of my visit read:

> The one-room cabin with its puncheon floor, a stone fireplace with oven at one end, and primitive furniture is an authentic reproduction of the type of dwelling built by the earliest settlers in the Western Reserve [the region of northeastern Ohio that had been "reserved" for settlers from Connecticut, leading to a quasi-New England feel to the area]. The utensils shown are all originals, some dating as early as the 18th Century (see Figure P.1).

Wow, that said it all, I thought. A basic log cabin, with its primitive "puncheon" floor (whatever that was, but it sounded sturdy and hand hewn); a fireplace for cooking, no doubt, hearty meals; and authentic objects—some dating back two centuries! All the elements in this room were as different as night and day from the comfortable 1950s-era suburban house that I called home. Yet somehow I could relate. Maybe it was that mannequin of the woman wearing pioneer clothes in the back corner of the room. But I had a feeling that it was more than that. Whatever it was, I felt transported into that room, into that world, a world in which that woman churned butter in that butter churn, spun flax on that spinning wheel, cooked soups and stews in

**Figure P.1.    Postcard of the Pioneer Log Cabin at the Western Reserve Historical Society, Cleveland, Ohio, purchased on a school field trip by the author**
Courtesy of the author

those pots and kettles, ground herbs inside that mortar and pestle, and rocked her baby in that cradle.

But wait. This wasn't real. As the postcard said, it was an "authentic reproduction." I knew from the beginning that it wasn't real. But it didn't seem to matter. It came alive, let my imagination soar, led—in some way, I believe—to a lifelong interest in and career of studying how people carried out their daily lives in the past, how that connects and resonates with us today, and what we can learn from that.

With my anthropology background from college and interest in material culture studies, I was accepted into a prestigious graduate program—the Winterthur Program in Early American Culture.[1] Most of the students went there to learn the finer points of connoisseurship by studying high-style furniture. But I spent much of my time steeping in the ordinary stuff of everyday life. My research on historic kitchens helped me land my first job—as a curatorial assistant at The Henry Ford, in Dearborn, Michigan, working on that museum's one-of-a-kind collection of household equipment and utensils.[2]

That first summer in 1977, I was quite overwhelmed. Seemingly endless rows of washing machines, cookstoves, and refrigerators; shelf upon shelf of egg beaters, apple parers, cherry pitters, coffee grinders—all needing research, cataloging, and selecting for an upgraded exhibit to commemorate Henry Ford Museum's fiftieth anniversary in 1979. To my delight, one of my

**Figure P.2.** 1890s kitchen in the series of four historic kitchen environments, Henry Ford Museum of American Innovation, Dearborn, Michigan
Photo by Deborah Berk

first tasks was to recreate four historic kitchen spaces, to compare and contrast their change through time from the eighteenth century to the 1930s (see Figure P.2). It was hard work, I discovered. I had no real methodology other than finding objects that matched the scant images I found in books and then writing a label explaining each kitchen. Our exhibit designer, thank goodness, suggested wall and flooring materials and colors. What did I know about that? I was an object curator.

I didn't feel like those four kitchens seemed very believable or that I'd done a very good job. But visitors seemed to like them. They spent long periods of time in front of them, talking excitedly among themselves and pointing a lot. I heard several people exclaim things like "Grandma had one of those!" I even used that phrase in the title of one of my lectures, rather derisively. What I didn't understand was why they were so excited about those kitchens, why those kitchens brought up so many of their own personal memories, and why so few of them read my very erudite (I thought) labels. I clearly had a lot to learn about visitors. In fact, they were going through just what I had gone through with that pioneer kitchen when I was younger: using their imaginations to construct a narrative about what they were seeing and then connecting it to their own lives.

Over the past forty years, I have learned much more about visitors—particularly through the discipline of visitor studies—as well as honing my skills in both historical research and storytelling techniques and in aligning both of these with institutional mission, vision, and project goals. For me, it was always about the presence of people. Those period rooms. Those immersive spaces. Those environments that attempted to recreate a past time and place. Why did I care? Why should others care? I have come to think that these connections are at the core of what makes us human. They ground us, define and confirm our human-ness, help us see our world and our place in it with more clarity, understanding, and insight. Our role in creating these environments—knowing the power they innately have over people yet also knowing they can never truly be the real thing—is to do the very best job we can of combining proven strategies and techniques that come from many disciplines. That is what this book is about.

## THE CASE STUDIES

To give a sense of how the methodology laid out in this book translates into real-world practice, three relevant case studies are referenced throughout the steps, described in chapters 3 through 6. These case studies, developed and refined over the past few decades by the author, serve as teaching tools for the entire process, from conceptual planning through historical research to creating and interpreting the final environment. The case studies include:

- The log home birthplace of William Holmes McGuffey (in Greenfield Village), originally from southeastern Pennsylvania; date of interpretation: 1800 to 1802.
- The J. R. Jones General Store (in Greenfield Village), originally from Waterford, Michigan; date of interpretation: 1882 to 1888.
- A "Back-to-the-Land" Commune environment in the *Your Place in Time: 20th Century America* exhibition (in Henry Ford Museum of American Innovation), date of interpretation: 1973.

## CHAPTER DESCRIPTIONS

Chapter 1, "The Power of Immersion in Historical Environments," explores the multidisciplinary scholarship that helps to explain the powerful feeling of immersion that occurs when visitors experience historical environments. This chapter begins by focusing on six factors of immersion experiences that social science researcher Stephen Bitgood, after undertaking numerous studies, has concluded seem most salient in creating the feeling of immersion in these environments. These factors, in fact, draw from a wide spectrum of disciplines, including psychology, philosophy, literary studies, public history, education, and narratology (i.e., the ways in which a narrative structures our perception of the world). Bitgood's six factors are discussed in more depth within the context of each of these disciplines and as they relate specifically to museums. This section is followed by an exploration into the "so what" factor—that is, the potential value and benefits of historical environments to visitors and to the museums that create them—drawing from scholarly work in formal education, free-choice learning in museums, experiential learning, and several emerging topics in museums grouped together under what one researcher has referred to as "beyond learning." Finally, a few cautions in creating historical environments are called out, as they relate to any attempt by museums to recreate and interpret the past.

In the preface to this book, I argue that the most engaging and memorable historical environments involve a creative integration of historical accuracy and a cohesive, unified narrative. These two key elements have emerged from different disciplinary worlds. Chapter 2, "Pioneering Contributions to Historical Environments," offers foundational case studies that exemplify each of these. For story-based environments, the seminal works of architect Mary Colter and visionary animator, entrepreneur, and theme park creator Walt Disney are explored. The integration of cross-disciplinary methodologies by the so-called new social historians into early living history environments—as exemplified by the interior settings at Old World Wisconsin—offers a contrasting case study. Each of these pioneering contributors brought their unique background, vision, and approach to creating historical environments, but they also share some commonalities. Our deeper understanding of both their differences and similarities helps us determine how to draw out their most useful lessons and begin to integrate them together.

Chapter 3, "Framing Your Project," begins to lay out the process for creating historical environments. Taking the time to engage in this early planning process will ensure that a firm rationale is established for everything that follows, including creating the environments. More often than not, historical environments constitute discreet components of larger exhibition projects, whereas they can encompass an entire historic structure or site. Therefore, although there are many overlaps, these are described separately in this chapter. Checklists for developing these environments are included. The early planning processes from two case studies—the 1973 "Back-to-the-Land" Commune environment in the *Your Place in Time: 20th Century America* exhibition and the J. R. Jones General Store—are described here as real-world examples.

Chapter 4, "Your Research Methodology," continues to describe the process for creating historical environments. Several times in the process—usually near the beginning and later on—you will be engaging in rigorous and systematic historic research. In this chapter, you will learn how to begin this research by asking relevant questions and then continue the process by identifying and analyzing different sources that address these questions. Each of the kinds of sources described here inherently possesses pros and cons, which are described and then summarized in a table. The discussion of different types of sources is followed by an in-depth description of the research methodology applied to three discrete case studies: the log home birthplace of William Holmes McGuffey (interpreted 1800–1802), the J. R. Jones General Store (interpreted 1882–1888), and the "Back-to-the-Land" Commune environment in the *Your Place in Time: 20th Century America* exhibition (interpreted 1973).

Chapter 5, "Bringing Your Environment to Life," begins by describing how to combine your conceptual framework and historical research with story elements to create a backstory that adds the people into your environment in ways that are both historically plausible and emotionally compelling. The backstory lays the foundation for the more familiar steps that follow—an interpretive strategy and a furnishings plan. Each of these steps is elucidated with real-life examples from the three case studies described above. This chapter also includes a checklist for creating a backstory and a table of strengths and weaknesses for considering different interpretive techniques.

After determining the conceptual framework, completing the historical research, and developing an interpretive strategy and furnishings plan for your environment, you have reached the point of actually creating the environment. Chapter 6, "At Last! Creating Your Environment," will explain how to write a visitor experience walkthrough, experiment with layouts, and complete the actual installation. Strategies for training interpreters to communicate your vision and developing a written interpretive manual for their reference are also described here, along with post-opening evaluation and ongoing attention to maintenance and refinement. These steps are elucidated through the three case studies included in this book. A checklist for creating a visitor experience walkthrough and an actual walkthrough excerpt are included here.

The final chapter of this book features descriptions of historical environments from several other museums. Described in their entirety from concept to visitor experience to impact, these suggest the range and possibilities of environments that can be created in museums of varying size and scope. A wrap-up of common threads that helps explain the popularity and success of these environments leads us full circle back to the power of immersion in historical environments that is described in chapter 1.

My hope is that the strategies and examples offered in *Spaces That Tell Stories: Recreating Historical Environments* will not only help you plan and/ or reenvision the historical environments at your own institutions, but also convince others that this is necessary and important work. Numerous benefits await in creating these environments—for staff, for visitors, for stakeholders, for your community, and, finally, for yourself. Countless people I talked to during the creation of this book who worked on these types of environments at their own institutions said, "That was my favorite project ever!" I feel that way as well. The challenging yet highly creative and deeply satisfying nature of these projects sparks in us the passion we bring to our work every day. That's truly why I wrote this book.

## NOTES

1. Now called the Winterthur Program in American Material Culture, this is a joint program between the University of Delaware in Newark, Delaware, and the Henry Francis du Pont Winterthur Museum. For more on this program, see https://www .winterthur.org/education/academic-programs/graduate-degree-program/american -material-culture/.

2. The scope of this combined indoor and outdoor complex is massive, with numerous exhibitions and historic structures covering more than 300 years of the American experience. In 1977, it included Henry Ford Museum and Greenfield Village. Today, The Henry Ford encompasses the renamed Henry Ford Museum of American Innovation, Greenfield Village, Ford Rouge Factory Tour, and the Benson Ford Research Center. See https://www.thehenryford.org/ for more information.

# Acknowledgments

I have often likened The Henry Ford—the museum at which I have worked for more than four decades—to a city. As such, there are too many colleagues, both past and present, to acknowledge each one individually for contributing ideas that somehow made their way into this book. I would, however, like to acknowledge the influence, encouragement, and inspiration of past colleague Gretchen Overhiser and long-time colleague Jeanine Head Miller in the creation of this book. I also thank Jeanine as well as other staff members from The Henry Ford—John Neilson, Katherine White, Saige Jedele, Ryan Jelso, and Andy Stupperich—for reviewing and commenting upon the manuscript of this book; to Jim Orr for his help supplying images from The Henry Ford's collections; and to Marc Greuther for supporting my writing of this book.

Sometimes, people come into your life unexpectedly, and, fairly quickly, you realize that they are kindred spirits. This was true of long-time friend and colleague Larry Fisher—a designer, experience developer, and one-time Disney Imagineer, who was, among other things, instrumental in envisioning the *Your Place in Time* exhibition—and more recent acquaintance, designer Brad Thiel, whom I learned had designed many of my favorite exhibitions at the Minnesota History Center. A special thanks to both of them for helping shape and reinforce my ideas during the writing of this book.

Thank you to the many colleagues and acquaintances at other museums who willingly (and even enthusiastically!) took the time to fill out my in-depth questionnaire, agreed to in-person or telephone conversations, or answered questions via email for the last chapter of this book. These contributors were Daniel Goodman (El Rancho de Las Golondrinas); Megan Wood (Ohio History Connection); Christian Carron and Jennifer Robinson (Children's Museum of Indianapolis); Jesse Heinzen (Minnesota Historical Society); Christopher Wilson (Split Rock Studios); John Herbst (Indiana

Historical Society); Mick Woodcock (Sharlot Hall Museum); Claire Rogers, Krystal Willeby, Matt Driggers, and Chris Godbold (George Ranch); Sarah Bartlett (previously on the staff at Split Rock Studios, now an independent consultant); Michelle Moon (Tenement Museum); and Melissa Peterson (Lindbergh House and Museum). Because of their assistance, I feel that this chapter offers a new, unique, and invaluable contribution to the museum field. Thanks also to John Goodson at the Children's Museum of Indianapolis for responding to my questions via email about that museum's cultural sensitivity and inclusivity training. Special thanks to John Herbst, who not only filled out a questionnaire for me but also graciously agreed to write the Foreword to this book. Additional thanks to Daniel Goodman, Megan Wood, Christian Carron, Jesse Heinzen, Christopher Wilson, and John Herbst for generously supplying images.

Thanks to old friends Tom Kelleher at Old Sturbridge Village and Dan Freas at Old World Wisconsin, who responded to my call for images from our earlier days in the living history field, and to Caitlin Emery Avenia (Old Sturbridge Village) and Catherine L. Dallas (Old World Wisconsin) for graciously following up with historical images from these sites. Thanks also to Caroline Braden and Elaine Kaiser for generously allowing me to use photographs they had taken. A special acknowledgment to lifetime friend, photographer, and artist Deborah Berk for making a special trip from New York City to take photographs for this book for me, patiently listening as I explained my reasoning behind the need for each one.

Thank you to Rowman & Littlefield Publishing Group's executive editor, Charles Harmon, who kept encouraging me to write a book proposal until I finally hit upon the one for this book (I don't know how it took me so long!) and for offering helpful comments during the writing of this manuscript; also to editorial assistant Michael Tan for his quick responses to my numerous technical and logistical questions. Additional thanks to the staff at AASLH for supporting the publication of this book. I would also like to thank Judith Endelman, Brad Taylor, and Tim Neill for their advice and encouragement when I was transitioning from a simple book proposal to a real book.

Finally, I could never have written this book without the patience and support of my husband, Curt, and daughter, Caroline, who listened while I talked through my ideas, chapter by chapter, and allowed me to disappear for days at a time to write.

**1**

# The Power of Immersion in Historical Environments

Some museum scholars and professionals might declare that historical environments are out of step with the times, perhaps even obsolete. They might claim that visitors these days want flashy media, sophisticated technology interactives, or the latest immersion techniques like Augmented or Virtual Reality. Or, they might argue that these environments don't present STEM principles or don't align with traditional learning objectives.[1] Yet, as social science researcher Stephen Bitgood maintained in his study of immersion experiences, the number and popularity of these experiences suggest that there is something of value in them to those who seek them out.[2] I would argue that there are numerous benefits to both visitors and the museums who create them. The impact and benefits of creating and interpreting these environments (along with a few cautions) constitute the core of this chapter.

## THE IMPACT OF IMMERSION EXPERIENCES

I like how, when you look at a display, it feels like you could be there.[3]

[The immersive setting includes] a lot of things that I've seen in history books, things that bring it more to life. That's worth a lot more than just reading . . . words on a piece of paper.[4]

Respondents felt that their lives had become so crazy, so complicated, so unreal that they were seeking an authentic respite from an unreal world. They want to feel they are "in that period of time and [can] forget the world today."[5]

Although these visitor comments were collected at different times and places, the verdict is still the same. Historical environments grab ahold of people, elicit emotional responses, and stay in people's memories longer than many other aspects of museum visits. Clearly, something active and powerful is going on. But what exactly is it? And, once we know that, how can we harness the power of these environments to enhance their value to visitors while also furthering the mission, vision, and strategic goals of our institutions?

Stephen Bitgood's in-depth study and analysis of immersion experiences provide perhaps the best insight into the dynamics between these experiences and museum visitors.[6] After numerous studies testing different aspects of visitor behavior in these spaces, Bitgood concluded that six factors, in particular, seem particularly important in creating the feeling of immersion:

- "Realism of the illusion"—the degree to which an environment creates the illusion of time and place; how real or "authentic" it seems.
- "Dimensionality"—the use of a setting or physical space to create an engaging, cohesive environment. The higher the degree of perceptual depth, Bitgood found, the greater the feeling of immersion.
- "Multisensory stimulation"—the presence of sensory impressions beyond visuals, including sound, smell, texture, light, and temperature. The more senses that are involved, Bitgood concluded, the greater the feeling of immersion.
- "Mental imagery"—the degree to which visitors can picture "in their mind's eye" something beyond what is actually there.
- "Lack of interfering factors"—the absence of sights, sounds, and other details that are incompatible with the intended setting.
- "Meaningfulness"—the degree to which the subject matter comes to life, attracts the visitor's interest and attention, and is easily understandable.[7]

These six factors, in actuality, draw from a wide spectrum of disciplines, including psychology, philosophy, literary studies, public history, education, and narratology (i.e., the ways in which a narrative structures our perception of the world). The following elaborates upon these disciplinary perspectives, revealing even greater insight into just what is going on when visitors experience a historical environment.

### Realism of the Illusion

Bitgood wrote that "It has been argued that authenticity is a major theme underlying human behavior."[8] As museum professionals, we generally take for granted the concept of authenticity. This, of course, implies both rigorous research and real things—or at least accurately researched recreations of these things. But what does this concept mean to museum visitors who might be viewing a historical environment? In a broad-based study of more than 5,000 museum visitors, the research and predictive analytics firm Reach Advisors found that many respondents equated authenticity with "stepping back in time and immersing myself in the past."[9] Authenticity, to them, involved "real people, real stories, [and] accurate representations of real lives." Many respondents also felt that authenticity was conveyed through a cohesive, unified, and accurately portrayed experience.[10]

Artifacts seem to be particularly powerful in conveying a sense of authenticity to visitors. Indeed, in their classic book, *The Presence of the Past*, historians Roy Rosenzweig and David Thelen reported that the respondents in their study felt that artifacts were direct links to the past, allowing people to imagine experiencing that time and place without mediation (see Figure 1.1).[11] Real things, cohesive experiences, accurate portrayals of the past—all these characteristics add authenticity to the immersion experiences that Bitgood studied.

**Figure 1.1.** The concept of authenticity plays a major role in the immersion experience when visitors enter La Tiendita ("the little store") at El Rancho de las Golondrinas in Santa Fe, New Mexico.
Courtesy of El Rancho de las Golondrinas Living History Museum, Santa Fe, New Mexico

## Dimensionality

In psychology, dimensionality refers to how we perceive and recognize things in the three-dimensional world around us—sometimes referred to as environmental perception.[12] This involves taking in clues about the world around us through our senses, which, in turn, link to our thought processes, emotions, and memories.

Environmental perception also influences the time and energy we decide to devote to something. If something in our environment is uninteresting to us, hard to understand, or too confusing or complicated, chances are we will not devote the effort to further exploration. What motivates visitors to spend time and energy exploring an environment? In their benchmark studies of human behavior in environmental settings, psychologists Stephen and Rachel Kaplan found that people prefer settings that involve:

- Coherence—they "hang together" or are organized in an understandable way.
- Legibility—they have a degree of distinctiveness; the viewer can understand and categorize the contents.
- Complexity—there are a number and variety of different elements.
- Mystery—they contain hidden information to which the viewer is drawn.[13]

It would follow that successful historical environments—that is, those that most grab and hold visitors' attention—likely involve at least some of the above factors described in the Kaplans' study (see Figure 1.2).

Figure 1.2. This recreated Japanese internment camp barracks at Heart Mountain Interpretive Center, near Cody, Wyoming, embodies the concept of "dimensionality"— the furnishings and their arrangements are recognizable yet varied, complex, and a bit mysterious.
Courtesy of Christopher K. Wilson

## Multisensory Stimulation

In their book *Experiential Learning: A Handbook for Education, Training and Coaching*, learning specialists Colin Beard and John P. Wilson argue that the senses are our means of contact and communication with the outside world.[14] We transform individual bits of sensory data into the language of our brains and minds and learn to make them meaningful to ourselves.[15]

Why is multisensory stimulation so effective in creating a feeling of immersion in history museums? In their insightful essays, museum scholars Daniel Spock and D. Lynn McRainey offer some clues. In his article, "A Practical Guide to Personal Connectivity," Spock explains that the effect of "being plunged" into a place—"redolent with odors, tactile sensations, sights and sounds"—intensifies the emotional impact dramatically.[16] Expanding upon this in her essay, "A Sense of the Past," McRainey argues that the senses are a universal language that extends beyond the written word and reaches across boundaries of age, ability, gallery display cases, and even time. "As an interpretive tool for a history museum," she argues, "the senses stimulate emotions and memories, extend access to unfamiliar places and times, and invite participation."[17] "Through the senses," she concludes, "the past becomes accessible to the newcomer and is filled with unexpected possibilities."[18] (See Figure 1.3.)

Figure 1.3.   At the entrance to the "Get to the Basement!" experience in the *Weather Permitting* exhibition at the Minnesota History Center, the whirling and whooshing tornado, the scenes of disarray and destruction, and the loud sounds coming from behind the wall all hint at the multisensory experience to come.
Courtesy of Minnesota Historical Society

## Mental Imagery

Psychologists recognize that mental imagery—that is, the ability to picture something in one's "mind's eye"—is connected to perception, memory, thinking, and imagining. But how all this works has been the subject of debate for as long as humans have been trying to understand their own cognitive processes.[19] It dates at least as far back as the ancient Greek philosopher Aristotle, who referred to mental images as *phantasmata*, literally meaning "reflections in mirrors or pools."[20] Through various eras of psychological thought, the creation, existence, and functioning of mental imagery was contentiously debated; only in the past 50 years has the concept of mental representation been firmly established as central and vital to mental processes and to human consciousness in general (see Figure 1.4).[21]

Figure 1.4.   Visitors use "mental imagery" to picture the people who might have inhabited this 1973 "Back-to-the-Land" Commune environment from the *Your Place in Time* exhibition, Henry Ford Museum of American Innovation.
Photo by Deborah Berk

## Lack of Interfering Factors

The ability to achieve this end (i.e., to completely remove incompatible details) relates to a literary device that poet Samuel Taylor Coleridge coined way back in 1817: "that willing suspension of disbelief for the moment, which constitutes poetic faith."[22] Long before we could infer how the brain might support this puzzling phenomenon, Coleridge asked readers of his poem *The Rime of the Ancient Mariner* to accept the various premises that he laid out in the story and trust that they would all make sense in the end.[23] In more modern times, the authors of literary works like *Lord of the Rings* and the Harry Potter series ask readers to trust them in much the same way. Why does the "willing suspension of disbelief" work? Many psychologists believe that humans are born with the ability to allow a story's artificial structures to create a real experience for them. By knowing that something is not real, we stop worrying about judging it. We just accept it, enjoy it, go along for the ride. We "lose ourselves in it." We feel "transported."[24] This links directly back to what visitors experience when viewing historical environments (see Figure 1.5).

**Figure 1.5.** Through the lack of interfering factors in the changing series of *You Are There* exhibits at Indiana Historical Society, Indianapolis, Indiana, visitors are encouraged to suspend their disbelief and engage in the moment. This scene, of an interpreter portraying Mrs. Kaplan, was from *You Are There 1950: Making a Jewish Home.*
Courtesy of the Indiana Historical Society

## Meaningfulness

I would argue that all the attributes of Bitgood's factor of "meaningfulness"—that is, the environment attracting the visitor's interest and attention as well as the subject matter coming to life and being easily understandable—become infinitely more achievable when the historical environment has a unifying structure. This means adapting the storyteller's flair for creating a coherent, believable, logical narrative into the creation of a three-dimensional environment. Why are the ideas of storytelling and narrative so powerful and effective? Radio personality Garrison Keillor tells us that "true stories open up a space into which the listener's own thoughts, feelings, and memories can flow and expand. They inspire internal dialog and thus ensure a real connection."[25] Drawing upon the discipline of narratology (i.e., the way in which narrative shapes our perceptions), museum scholar Leslie Bedford explains in her article "Storytelling: The Real Work of Museums":

> Stories are the most fundamental way we learn. They have a beginning, a middle, and an end. They teach without preaching, encouraging both personal reflection and public discussion. Stories inspire wonder and awe; they allow a listener to imagine another time and place, to find the universal in the particular, and to feel empathy for others. They preserve individual and collective memory and speak to both the adult and the child.[26]

Historical environments are most powerful when the story inherently emanates from the setting, using a minimum of mediation from us (that is, labels, live interpreters, and other forms of didactic explanation). How can we achieve maximum "meaningfulness" with minimum mediation? Museum exhibit designer Brad Thiel likens these environments to stage sets. In the same way a theater designer must consider the viewpoint from every seat in the house, Thiel recommends looking at these environments "from many possible perspectives."[27] Ask yourself, he advises, how does the environment create a space for family and group interaction? How does it support the emotional tone?

I believe that Walt Disney Imagineers provide the benchmark for exploring ways to successfully embed narrative and storytelling techniques into three-dimensional environments. This group of talented "imagination engineers," created by Walt Disney himself back in the 1950s, is responsible for developing the attractions and themed environments at Disney theme parks around the world. Joe Rohde, senior vice president, Creative, at Walt Disney Imagineering, calls this concept "narrative placemaking"—that is, the idea that a spatial environment can have the quality of narrative, full of implicit character, action, and plot.[28] Rohde suggests several strategies for achieving a narrative structure within spatial environments, including:

- Thematic unity, in that choosing a theme creates the sense of cohesion around which all subsequent decisions are made, including placement, sequence, and appearance of objects and other details.[29]
- Intuitive navigation, with each component constituting a unique statement that becomes part of the whole and all of them combining to create a cohesive narrative that makes sense without the need for additional didactic explanation like labels.[30]
- Nonlinear arrangement, important because a three-dimensional spatial environment is not sequential like a book, a movie, or a TV show, but all aspects of the experience must reiterate the core ideas that drive the story. As a result, visitors entering the experience at any point or from any direction must still be able to "get" the story.[31]

## BENEFITS OF HISTORICAL ENVIRONMENTS

Now that we have explored Bitgood's six factors of engaging immersion experiences and delved more deeply into the multidisciplinary origins of each of them, the question remains, so what? Is any learning happening? Is there other value to the dynamic between visitors and historical environments that benefits individuals, groups, or even society as a whole? The answer to these questions, I would argue, is an unqualified yes.

Scholarship in museum learning and studies in visitor behavior both help inform our understanding of the many potential benefits of historical environments. For example, Bitgood found in his studies that, under the right conditions, immersion can facilitate several types of learning, including:

- Declarative knowledge—verbal or written statements about the experience that relate to traditional academic objectives.
- Procedural knowledge—demonstrating how to use or do something.
- Spatial knowledge—understanding relationships within a spatial environment.[32]

Moreover, in a survey querying 144 museum professionals about immersive exhibitions, museum studies master's student Hallie Gilbert found that many of her respondents believed that these settings convey content effectively and that they "engage visitors more easily in the content."[33] One respondent remarked that, "Immersion is one way to allow visitors to learn in a variety of ways."[34] Another commented that "These exhibitions speak to many different audiences and provide the best environment for the widest array of learning to take place."[35]

Gilbert also admitted, however, that some museum professionals worry that, although immersive exhibitions are effective for their "greater holding power and memorability," they may not have enough educational value.[36] This raises the question of how one defines educational value. In response to this concern, Gilbert suggested that perhaps, rather than using traditional measures of knowledge acquisition, we should be asking questions like Do immersive exhibitions engender more sociability? Are they more memorable? Do they draw visitors? Do they attract different audiences? Do visitors return because of them?[37] Indeed, I would argue that if we are defining learning as simply the acquisition of facts, we are using an outmoded and irrelevant definition, particularly as it relates to the museum experience. Many museum scholars and professionals confirm this. As Daniel Spock wrote in "A Practical Guide to Personal Connectivity,"

> While we have tended to presuppose that learning is the chief motivating factor for our visitors, in truth this may only be one aspect of what they desire in their experience with us. This is especially the case if we define learning narrowly as limited to the acquisition of information. If we see learning more broadly defined as making meaningful connections (however visitors choose to do it), then we are in a better position to evaluate the effort.[38]

What Falk and Dierking have called "free-choice learning" in museum settings—that is, learning that is freely chosen, nonlinear, and personally motivated—is much more aligned with what occurs during the museum visit and is especially helpful in determining the benefits and value of historical environments.[39] Elements of free-choice learning that are particularly relevant here include the following.

## The Affective Experience, or Emotional Impact

Bitgood found in his studies that, to a larger or smaller degree, immersion experiences have "an affective impact" (evoking, for example, curiosity, excitement, or sadness) and that visitors experiencing them reported enhanced vividness and meaningfulness compared to "book learning."[40] In fact, learning research suggests that emotion is actually "a vital aspect of learning and problem solving and, consequently, it is an important dimension of any successful learning experience."[41] In their book *Experiential Learning*, Beard and Wilson confirm that affective experiences not only enhance one's own learning, but they can also help people develop increased sensitivity to self and others as well as more ability to think independently and challenge existing beliefs.[42]

## Memory

Bitgood's and others' studies suggest that historical environments are among the more memorable aspects of a museum visit. Many museum theorists find that memories from museum visits are, in fact, an integral part of free-choice learning. In their insightful article "Museum Memory," psychologists Douglas Herrman and Dana Plude suggest that a range of experiences and inputs during a museum visit lead to later recall, including objects, sensory impressions, environmental settings, talking with others, and personal reflection.[43] Any or all of these can encourage visitors to reflect upon their overall visit, categorize these impressions into existing experiences, and help them better understand themselves, others, and their place in the world.[44]

## Interest, Attention, and Flow

According to Gilbert's study, many museum professionals felt that immersive exhibitions have a strong ability to "capture the audience's attention and provide a highly memorable experience."[45] However, counter to the perception by some of Gilbert's respondents that capturing attention is *all* that occurs when visitors encounter these spaces, many museum theorists and professionals argue that it is precisely *because* of this factor that these environments can aid in the long-term retention of content. Museum specialist Ed Rodley argues that immersive environments don't simply attract attention; they actually provide a kind of flow experience where memorable learning can take place.[46] Psychologist Mihaly Csikszentmihalyi, who created the concept of flow, confirms that a flow experience is possible in museum experiences when goals are clear, feedback is unambiguous, and challenges and skills are well matched.[47] Within this state, Czikszentmihalyi maintains, sustained interest can inspire awe, deep emotional connections, a heightened sense of discovery, and a more extensive learning interaction.[48]

## "Experiential Learning"

This newer learning model has great potential for understanding the learning that occurs in museums and is especially relevant to assessing the impact of historical environments. In their book *Experiential Learning*, Beard and Wilson define this concept as "the sense-making process between the inner world of the person and the outer world of the environment."[49] Involving the "whole person," it is a process of active engagement with an experience through thoughts, feelings, and in some cases, physical activity.[50] Sensory awareness—which plays a major role in this process—not only enhances learning but, the authors maintain, "The more senses we use in an activity, the more memorable the learning experience will become because it increases the neural connections in our brains and therefore will make it more accessible."[51]

Experiential learning also sparks the imagination, which education theorist Kieran Egan and other researchers suggest is "a powerful avenue for learning and exploration."[52] Indeed, Beard and Wilson argue that "imagination is one of the most powerful mental tools we have at our disposal."[53] With imagination, they maintain, we can engage in "mental time travel," speculate possible alternatives, and select a course of action that can lead toward the achievement of our goals and objectives. Imagination helps us plan, hope, and dream, and it encourages empathy for others.[54]

## Personal Meaning-Making

The concept of personal meaning-making seems particularly salient in terms of the experience that occurs with historical environments. In her groundbreaking work on this topic, museum scholar Lois Silverman asserted that meaning-making is a basic human process, something we engage in all the time.[55] In museums, through a constant process of remembering and connecting, people attempt to place what they encounter within the context of their previous life experience (including special knowledge, expectations and norms, and life events and situations).[56] This is important to not only learning but also to our psychological well-being. Furthermore, it can provide opportunities to build upon, confirm, or encourage basic values, such as pride, respect, and tolerance.[57]

## Learning within a Social Context

Historical environments can provide a powerful benefit to the social experience of museum-going, as groups of people are often observed looking at and talking about these environments together. Museum researchers John Falk and Lynn Dierking argue that museum visitors build knowledge and understanding through conversation, gestures, and observation of others.[58] Silverman confirms that, in the social experience, the group produces a shared approach to the museum visit, drawing upon common history and knowledge of each other to fill in gaps, to learn new things, and to create content and meaning together.[59]

## Beyond Learning

Many studies confirm that museum experiences have benefits that transcend what has traditionally been considered learning, and the unique qualities of historical environments have the potential to play an important role in attaining these. For example, social science researcher Jan Packer, in her article "Beyond Learning," confirmed the essential role of two constructs that occur during museum visits: mental restoration and psychological well-being.[60] Both of these constructs, Packer argues, can improve the quality of life and enable individuals and communities to thrive rather than just survive.

Another major benefit of historical environments is the potential for empathy—that is, imagining standing in someone else's shoes, sharing another person's feelings, taking another person's perspective. The human capacity for empathy helps us make sense of the world, enabling and enriching our interactions with others, motivating altruistic behavior, and encouraging creativity.[61] Within a history museum context, Daniel Spock explains in his essay, "Imagination: A Child's Gateway to Engagement,"

> Having empathy helps us understand ourselves better by understanding others and our own place in our relationship with them. Visitors make constant comparisons between personal experience and the depicted experience of people in the past.[62]

A final benefit that reaches "beyond learning" is what anthropologist Nelson Graburn, in his groundbreaking 1977 article, "The Museum and the Visitor Experience," calls "reverential"—that is, the visitor's need for a personal experience with something higher, more sacred, and out of the ordinary than home and work are able to supply.[63] Building upon this concept, anthropologists Catherine M. Cameron and John B. Gatewood have confirmed the existence and value of what they call "the numinous experience" by visitors who connect on a spiritual level with historic sites.[64] More recently, museum scholar Kiersten F. Latham has drawn from the discipline of phenomenology to uncover deep spiritual connections between museum visitors and historic objects.[65]

## CAUTIONS IN CREATING HISTORICAL ENVIRONMENTS

At the same time that historical environments have the potential of numerous benefits, there are also cautions to keep in mind when creating and interpreting these environments. Similar to all our attempts to research and interpret the past, we should be aware of these possible pitfalls:

### It Is Impossible to Truly Know the Past

In discussing the significant role that museums play in telling Americans about their past, historical archaeologist James Deetz warned in his article "A Sense of Another World: History Museums and Cultural Change":

This past is ever subject to interpretation, and we will never be able to re-create it completely, with all of its subtleties and texture, or know the past as a participant in it might have done.[66]

## Stories Simplify the Past

Even though stories help unify history in engaging and memorable ways, they also bring additional cautions. In his classic book, *The Past Is a Foreign Country*, historical geographer David Lowenthal warned that, as the contingent and discontinuous facts of the past become intelligible only when woven together as stories, these make history seem more predictable and less complex than it actually was.[67]

## History Is Always Interpreted through the Present

No matter how we try to prevent it, the present always intrudes on our attempts to recreate the past. As Lowenthal wrote, we creatively change our portrayals of the past to make them convincing and intelligible in today's world, to align with current and constantly shifting values, perceptions, and needs.[68]

## Institutional Agendas

Historical environments are the product of institutional decision-making that might (and should) include mission, vision, strategic plans, goals, and resources. This immediately skews the presentation in any such environment and it should be made clear to visitors what was intended.

## Individual Biases

Individuals creating the environments bring their own biases and judgments, their own personal tastes, knowledge, sophistication, and research skills. It is important to remember that every historical environment was created by the subjective judgment of an individual or project team and, like institutional agendas, comes with some bias.

## Visitors Take Things Literally

While we museum professionals know we can never truly recreate the past, visitors generally assume that that is exactly what we are doing! As Rosenzweig and Thelen reported in *The Presence of the Past*, visitors find museums to be trustworthy purveyors of the truth.[69] When they see objects and settings, they assume that that is what life was really like. When they see costumed individuals "inhabiting" those spaces, they assume that that is how individuals in the past looked and acted.

## Details Are Too Subtle

Studies of visitors at historical environments reveal that they often miss or do not understand the details that museum professionals bring to them—to add atmosphere, to suggest the complexity of the past, or for any number of other reasons—and potentially miss major points that the individuals, project teams, or museums were intending to make.[70]

## Personal Meaning-Making

What was called out as a benefit is also mentioned here as a caution. Because visitors interpret these environments from their own perspective of personal meaning-making, they may take away an entirely different meaning of something than what the museum intended.[71]

## Uncomfortable History

Many respondents in the Reach Advisors study expressed mixed feelings about museums presenting difficult and uncomfortable issues of the past, like slavery, racism, and religious intolerance.[72] They want experiences that make them think deeply, but they also want museums to consider how their interpretation will affect children's and their own ability to confront these more complex issues.[73] As history museums debate and experiment with interpreting the more contentious issues of our past, as well as attempt to represent diversity and multiple perspectives, historical environments have the potential to serve as testing grounds for interpreting the past with greater accuracy and complexity, staging grounds for aiding in cultural healing and dialogue, or battlegrounds for contentious debate and disagreement.

What strategies can we use to attempt to counteract these cautions? First, do not assume that your visitors just "get it." It is crucial to find ways to clearly communicate your vision through interpretive strategies that best fit your goals, your budget, and the experience itself (see chapter 5 for a description of several possible interpretive strategies for historical environments). Second, do not just trust your own judgment. It is helpful to not only involve visitors, community members, and/or stakeholders from the outset to establish goals but also to check back with them later to see whether your goals have been successfully achieved. For example, as described in chapter 7, the design team for the Heart Mountain Interpretive Center worked with community stakeholders throughout the entire process to ensure that the recreated barracks in the Interpretive Center portrayed their ancestors' experience at this Japanese internment camp as accurately as possible. Also described in chapter 7, the planning team for *The Power of Children: Making a Difference* exhibition at the Children's Museum of Indianapolis decided to include traditional case displays outside the environment to ensure that visitors understood the context, while the team developing the *You Are There* exhibit galleries at the Indiana Historical Society decided to add not only case displays before visitors enter the environment but also have trained facilitators there to explain the time frame of each scene, the characters that visitors will encounter, and the activities in which visitors can engage once they enter the immersive space.

In handling environments that are potentially controversial, emotionally difficult, and/or sacred to some, it is even more important to both find acceptable ways to communicate your goals and to check back with visitors, community members, and/or stakeholders. There is a great deal of current literature on this topic, particularly as it relates to interpreting slavery.[74] Recommended strategies include working with expert advisers who can raise potential sensitivity and inclusion issues during the planning phase of the project and developing a formalized training program for visitor-facing staff that offers strategies and scenarios for dealing with sensitivity and inclusion issues.[75]

## THE IMPACT OF HISTORICAL ENVIRONMENTS

Using Stephen Bitgood's six factors of immersion experiences as a jumping-off point, this chapter delved into the multidisciplinary perspectives that help explain the power of historical environments for visitors to museums. These factors—which include realism of the illusion, dimensionality, multisensory stimulation, mental imagery, lack of interfering factors, and meaningfulness—in fact, have roots in such disciplines as psychology, philosophy, literary studies, public history, education, and narratology. Additional scholarship in both museum learning and what one researcher calls "beyond learning" reveals numerous benefits of historical environments to both visitors and museums, including traditional knowledge acquisition, emotional impact, memory retention, personal meaning-making, an enhanced social experience, mental restoration, psychological well-being, empathy, and a spiritual or "numinous" connection. Finally, a few cautions in creating these environments serve as a reminder that museums must be careful in any attempts to recreate and interpret the past.

In the preface to this book, I argue that the most engaging and memorable historical environments combine, at their essence, historical accuracy with a cohesive, unified narrative. How does one achieve both of these, let alone at the same time? The search for answers to these questions begins with the pioneers—the pioneers of historical environments, that is. Pioneers from two very different worlds—narrative placemaking (Walt Disney was more likely to call it "three-dimensional storytelling") and living history environments— are the main characters of the next chapter. These early groundbreakers forged paths upon which we still tread today.

## NOTES

1. For an example of a historical environment that *does* present STEM principles, see the description in chapter 7 of *You Are There 1939: Healing Bodies, Changing Minds* at the Indiana Historical Society.

2. Stephen Bitgood, *Engaging the Visitor: Designing Exhibits That Work* (Edinburgh: MuseumsEtc, 2014), 167.

3. "Points in Time" Summative Evaluation, Senator John Heinz History Center, Pittsburgh, PA, implemented by SLi (unpublished manuscript, 1997).

4. "Your Place in Time: 20th Century America" Summative Evaluation, The Henry Ford, Dearborn, MI, implemented by staff of The Henry Ford (unpublished manuscript, 2001).

5. Respondents in the study were asked why they visit outdoor history museums. Susie Wilkening and Erica Donnis, "Authenticity? It Means Everything," *History News* 63, no. 4 (Autumn 2008): 18.

6. Bitgood, *Engaging the Visitor*, see chapters in section entitled, "Immersion," pp. 166–279.

7. Ibid., 181–83.

8. Ibid., 213.

9. Wilkening and Donnis, "Authenticity?" 18–23.

10. Ibid., 19.

11. Roy Rosenzweig and David Thelen, *The Presence of the Past: Popular Uses of History in American Life* (New York: Columbia University Press, 1998), 106–7.

12. Paul A. Bell, Jeffrey D. Fisher, Andrew Baum, and Thomas C. Greene, *Environmental Psychology*, 3rd ed. (Fort Worth, TX: Holt Rinehart and Winston, 1990), 27.

13. Bitgood, *Engaging the Visitor*, 265–66; Bell, Fisher, Baum and Greene, *Environmental Psychology*, 48.

14. Colin Beard and John P. Wilson, *Experiential Learning: A Handbook for Education, Training and Coaching*, 3rd ed. (London: Kogan Page, 2013), 166.

15. Peter Jarvis, *International Dictionary of Adult and Continuing Education* (London, 1999), quoted in Beard and Wilson, *Experiential Learning*, 168.

16. Daniel Spock, "A Practical Guide to Personal Connectivity," *History News* 63, no. 4 (Autumn 2008): 16.

17. D. Lynn McRainey, "A Sense of the Past," in *Connecting Kids to History with Museum Exhibitions*, ed. D. Lynn McRainey and John Russick (Walnut Creek, CA: Left Coast Press, 2010), 165.

18. Ibid., 165.

19. "Mental Imagery," Stanford Encyclopedia of Philosophy website, November 18, 1997, with substantive revision September 12, 2014, accessed August 13, 2017, https://plato.stanford.edu/entries/mental-imagery/index.html.

20. Ibid.

21. Ibid.

22. Michael Mueller, "What Brain Activity Can Explain Suspension of Disbelief?" Question answered by Norman N. Holland, Scientific American website, January 1, 2014, accessed June 22, 2017, https://www.scientificamerican.com/article/what-brain-activity-can-explain-sus/.

23. Ibid.

24. Ibid.

25. Quoted in Leslie Bedford's "Working in the Subjunctive Mood: Imagination and Museums," Forum, *Curator* 47, no. 1 (January 2004): 5.

26. Leslie Bedford, "Storytelling: The Real Work of Museums," *Curator* 44, no. 1 (January 2001): 33.

27. Brad Thiel, email correspondence with author, April 19, 2018.

28. Joe M. Rohde, "Creating Narrative Space," *ICAM [International Confederation of Architectural Museums] 15*, Paris, session 4, 2nd of May 2010, 4, accessed September 13, 2017, http://www.icam-web.org/data/media/cms_binary/original/1284051324.pdf. See also Melody Malmberg, *The Making of Disney's Animal Kingdom Theme Park* (New York: Hyperion, 1998).

29. Ibid., 5.

30. Ibid., 8.

31. Ibid., 6–7.

32. Bitgood, *Engaging the Visitor*, 198.

33. Hallie Gilbert, "Immersive Exhibitions: What's the Big Deal?" *Visitor Studies Today!* 5, no. III (Fall 2002): 11.

34. Ibid., 11.

35. Ibid., 10–11.

36. Ibid., 10.

37. Ibid., 12–13.

38. Spock, "A Practical Guide to Personal Connectivity," 13.

39. John H. Falk and Lynn D. Dierking, *Learning from Museums: Visitor Experience and the Making of Meaning* (Walnut Creek, CA: AltaMira Press, 2000).

40. Bitgood, *Engaging the Visitor*, 198.

41. Institute for Learning Innovation, "'America on the Move'" Front-End Study, Best Practice Analysis," 18–25 (unpublished manuscript, September 2000).

42. Beard and Wilson, *Experiential Learning*, 189.

43. Douglas Herrman and Dana Plude, "Museum Memory," in *Public Institutions for Personal Learning: Establishing a Research Agenda*, ed. John Falk and Lynne D. Dierking (Washington, DC: AAM Technical Information Service, 1995), 57.

44. Herrman and Plude, "Museum Memory," 63.

45. Gilbert, "Immersive Exhibitions," 11.

46. Ed Rodley, "Tilting at Windmills, Part One," Thinking about Museums (blog), October 29, 2013, accessed August 13, 2017, http://exhibitdev.wordpress.com/2013/10/29/tilting-at-windmills-part-one/.

47. Mihaly Csikszentmihalyi and Kim Hermann, "Intrinsic Motivation in Museums: What Makes Visitors Want to Learn?" *Museum News* 74, no. 3 (May/June 1994): 35–37+. See also Mihaly Csikszentmihalyi and Kim Hermann, "Intrinsic Motivation in Museums: Why Does One Want to Learn?" in *Public Institutions for Personal Learning*.

48. Csikszentmihalyi and Hermann, "Intrinsic Motivation in Museums," 36.

49. Beard and Wilson, *Experiential Learning*, 26.

50. Ibid., 5.

51. Ibid., 9, 166.

52. Sharon Shaffer, "Never Too Young to Connect to History: Cognitive Development and Learning," in *Connecting Kids*, 44.

53. Beard and Wilson, *Experiential Learning*, 284.

54. Ibid., 284.

55. Lois H. Silverman's articles on meaning-making include "Visitor Meaning-Making in Museums for a New Age," *Curator* 38, no. 3 (1995): 161–70; "Taking a Wider View of Museum Outcomes and Experiences: Theory, Research, Magic," Madeleine Mainstone Lecture, *Journal of Education in Museums* 23 (2002): 3–8; and "Making Meaning Together: Lessons from the Field of American History," *Journal of Museum Education* 18, no. 3 (Fall 1993): 7–11. For other insightful articles on meaning-making, see "Meaning-Making in Museums," entire issue of *N.A.M.E. Exhibitionist* 18, no. 2 (Fall 1999) and "Meaning-Making Revisited," entire issue of *N.A.M.E. Exhibitionist* 32, no. 3 (Spring 2013).

56. Silverman, "Visitor Meaning-Making," 162.

57. Silverman, "Taking a Wider View," 234.

58. Falk and Dierking, *Learning from Museums*, 38.

59. Silverman, "Visitor Meaning-Making," 163.

60. Jan Packer, "Beyond Learning: Exploring Visitors' Perceptions of the Value and Benefits of Museum Experiences," *Curator* 51, no. 1 (January 2008): 33–54. See also Stephen Kaplan, Lisa V. Bardwell, and Deborah B. Slakter, "The Museum as a Restorative Environment," *Environment and Behavior* 25, no. 6 (1993): 725–42, accessed September 21, 2008, http://eab.sagepub.com/cgi/content/abstract/25/6/725.

61. For more on this topic, see the many interesting essays in the book *Fostering Empathy Through Museums*, ed. Elif M. Gokcigdem (Lanham, MD: Rowman & Littlefield, 2016).

62. Spock, "Imagination: A Child's Gateway to Engagement with the Past," in *Connecting Kids to History*, 128.

63. Nelson Graburn, "The Museum and the Visitor Experience," in *Museum Education Anthology: Perspectives on Informal Learning a Decade of Roundtable Reports, 1973–1983*, ed. Susan K. Nichols, Mary Alexander, and Ken Yellis (Washington, DC: Museum Education Roundtable, 1984), 180.

64. Catherine M. Cameron and John B. Gatewood, "Excursions into the Unremembered Past: What People Want from Visits to Historic Sites," *The Public Historian* 22, no. 3 (Summer 2000): 107–27.

65. Latham's articles include "The Poetry of the Museum: A Holistic Model of Numinous Museum Experiences," *Museum Management and Curatorship* 22, no. 3 (September 2007): 247–63; "Numinous Experiences with Museum Objects," *Visitor Studies* 16, no. 1 (2013): 3–20; and *The Objects of Experience: Transforming Visitor-Object Encounters in Museums*, with Elizabeth Wood (Walnut Creek, CA: Left Coast Press, 2014).

66. James Deetz, "A Sense of Another World: History Museums and Cultural Change," *Museum News* 58, no. 5 (May/June 1980): 40.

67. David Lowenthal, *The Past Is a Foreign Country* (Cambridge: University of Cambridge University Press, 1985), 218.

68. Ibid., 217.

69. Rosenzweig and Thelen, *The Presence of the Past*, 105.

70. Bitgood, *Engaging the Visitor*, 218. See also Judith Larsen, "To Label or Not—Visitors Win: New Life for an Immersion Exhibit," *Visitor Studies Today!* (Summer 2002): 11–16.

71. Silverman, "Making Meaning Together," 231.

72. Wilkening and Donnis, "Authenticity?" 20.

73. Ibid., 20.

74. Further reading on this topic includes the numerous insightful essays in Julia Rose's *Interpreting Difficult History at Museums and Historic Sites* (Lanham, MD: Rowman & Littlefield/AASLH, 2016) and in *Interpreting African American History and Culture at Museums and Historic Sites*, ed. Max van Balgooy (Lanham, MD: Rowman & Littlefield/AASLH, 2015); Kristin L. Gallas and James DeWolf Perry, "Developing Comprehensive and Conscientious Interpretation of Slavery at Historic Sites and Museums," *History News* 69, no. 2 (Spring 2014): Technical Leaflet #226; and "National Summit on Teaching Slavery," the report of a convening of national experts organized by James Madison's Montpelier and the National Trust for Historic Preservation, 2018, James Madison's Montpelier website, accessed January 4, 2019, https://www.montpelier.org/learn/tackling-difficult-history.

75. For example, in developing its *Power of Children: Making a Difference* exhibition, the Children's Museum of Indianapolis (described in chapter 7) not only received guidance from expert advisers on the best methods for presenting controversial and difficult topics for families and children but also developed a formalized training program for visitor-facing staff in the exhibition. Drawing from resources in conflict resolution and multicultural education, this "cultural sensitivity and inclusivity training" includes talking points, tips, and techniques for staff that incorporates overall strategies, procedures for handling visitors who are concerned about the exhibition's subject matter, and a participatory workshop for understanding personal biases, entitled "Lenses: Encouraging Cultural Sensitivity and Inclusivity." Email correspondence with John Goodson, Humanities Gallery Interpretation Manager, Children's Museum of Indianapolis, August 21, 2018, and February 1, 2019.

# 2

## Pioneering Contributions to Historical Environments

As I suggest in the preface to this book, the most engaging and memorable historical environments involve both historical accuracy and a cohesive, unified narrative. Unfortunately, combining these together is neither easy nor straightforward. Achieving a high degree of historical accuracy requires the rigorous analysis of data from primary-source documents, whereas developing a compelling narrative draws from the imagination and aims to convince people to suspend disbelief. These come from radically divergent disciplines, use different methodologies, and exist in separate worlds. But understanding each of them through a series of foundational case studies can help us determine how to draw out their most useful lessons and begin to integrate them together.

This chapter explores the work of significant pioneering contributors to historical environments. For story-based environments, the seminal works of architect Mary Colter and visionary animator, entrepreneur, and theme park creator Walt Disney are explored. The integration of cross-disciplinary methodologies by the so-called new social historians into early living history environments—as exemplified by the interior settings at Old World Wisconsin—offers a contrasting case study. While the approaches, goals, and philosophies of these contributors are admittedly different, deeper exploration of their work reveals surprising commonalities. Taken together, the contributions of these pioneers provide both lessons and models that are still relevant today.

### MARY COLTER, ARCHITECT IN THE SOUTHWEST

Mary Colter is a little-known figure in the museum world. But she shouldn't be. A female architect working in a world of men, she stands out as one of the earliest proponents of story-based historical environments.

Mary Elizabeth Jane Colter was born in 1869.[1] Her family moved around several times when she was young, finally settling in St. Paul, Minnesota. She expressed an early interest in art and, with her strong and determined personality, finally convinced her parents to send her to the California School of Design in San Francisco, citing as a reason that this school graduated students with the credentials to teach. There, she learned from top-notch architects of the day and apprenticed under a local architect at a time when certified architects were few and far between. Moreover, it was almost unprecedented for a woman to express interest in this field. But Mary was different. She dreamed of designing buildings that reflected the West and Southwest, inspired by the Spanish Mission–style architecture then in vogue in California. Upon graduation, she returned to St. Paul and did indeed teach—for the next fifteen years!

In 1902, her career dramatically changed when she was hired by the Fred Harvey Company—known for its high-standard Harvey House restaurants, hotels, and gift shops along the Atchison, Topeka & Santa Fe (AT&SF) Railroad route. Based upon her reputation as a "decorator who knew Indian things and had imagination," her first job was to artfully arrange the so-called Indian Building, a shop selling Native American handicrafts next to the new Alvarado Hotel in Albuquerque, New Mexico.[2] Thus began a forty-year association between Mary Colter, the Fred Harvey Company, and the AT&SF Railroad. Especially well-known were her many unique structures and interiors at the Grand Canyon, including Hopi House (1905), Hermit's Rest and Lookout Studio (1914), Phantom Ranch (1922), The Watchtower at Desert View (1932), and the interior at the Bright Angel Lodge (1935).[3]

According to Arnold Berke in *Mary Colter: Architect of the Southwest*, Colter's works "are beguiling stage sets rooted so masterfully in the history of the region that they seem to be genuine remnants of that history."[4] In fact, Colter increasingly found that she "could not visualize the design of a building or plan its decoration until she had thought out its 'history.'"[5] It is the creation of this "history" that is particularly relevant to our understanding of her pioneering contributions to historical environments.

Two of Colter's buildings, in particular, exemplify this and are used here as case studies: Hermit's Rest at the Grand Canyon, completed in 1914, and La Posada, a Fred Harvey resort hotel on the AT&SF Railroad line in Winslow, Arizona, completed in 1930. For each of these settings, Colter created a story, an actual narrative whose details she kept in mind as she made every decision—from overall design to materials and colors, from interior floor plan to furnishings and individual vignettes. As a result, in these two places, visitors are transported to another world of time and place, a world that is slowly revealed by looking in every direction, by absorbing every detail.

Hermit's Rest, intended as a rest area for tourists at the west end of the Grand Canyon's South Rim, cleverly evokes the retreat of a pioneer recluse. Although likely referencing an actual hermit who lived nearby, in Colter's own narrative,

> the structure was the remote dwelling of an old-time prospector who cobbled it together with materials he found around him. The old place had somehow survived long enough to welcome a new type of sojourner, the weary tourist.[6]

Every detail hones to this story. It is not only situated upon the edge of the canyon's rim, it appears as if it has grown organically out of the canyon. A lantern beckons visitors to make their way under the entrance arch, which is created of haphazardly piled stones. A long out-of-use mission bell is also positioned here, looking as if it was salvaged and brought to the site. The porch furniture is handmade, of twisted tree stumps with seats or tabletops hastily added. Inside the structure, the focal point is a massive fireplace with a stone arch (see Figure 2.1). Wrought iron wall candelabras, hanging metal lanterns, chairs from hollowed-out logs, and medieval-looking andirons help complete the scene of this recluse's retreat. The overall effect gives visitors

**Figure 2.1.   The Grand Fireplace at Hermit's Rest, Grand Canyon, designed by Mary Colter, circa 1916**
Credit: National Park Service

the feeling that this structure has been around a very long time, that a real person created it and might return at any moment, and that they themselves are now welcome to enjoy it.

La Posada was Colter's largest undertaking and, of all her buildings, it was "closest to her heart."[7] Here, she created her grandest and most elaborate narrative. According to the story that Colter fashioned, this hotel had once been Rancho La Posada, the residence of a wealthy Spanish gentleman and his family. A century earlier when this region was part of Mexico, it had been one of the largest *ranchos* of the Southwest. Deepening her story, Colter imagined that this *rancho* had been enlarged over the years by successive generations of the family so that it was now a large, rambling structure, with arched openings, arcaded walks, long *portales* (entryways), wrought iron window grilles and balcony railings, and a tile roof. The interior was outfitted with a mix of sophisticated and crude furnishings—elegant treasures that family members might have brought back from their travels juxtaposed with pieces that might have been fashioned by unskilled workers on the *rancho*. La Posada sat on eight acres of land, filled with broad lawns, orchards, and gardens, including a sunken garden with hidden shrines and a fountain off the patio. Its front faced the railroad tracks, inviting weary passengers to avail themselves of its cool, shaded grounds and calm, unhurried pace.

Based upon her work at Hermit's Rest and La Posada, what can we take away from Mary Colter's pioneering efforts at storytelling in three-dimensional environments?

1. Steep yourself in the history of the time and place related to the environment you are creating. Get to know the era, the place, the people who might have inhabited a space like this, their background, attitudes, and mindset. Put yourself in their shoes.
2. Align all your details—including materials, colors, lighting, and furnishings—with the narrative you have created so that wherever visitors look, whatever they experience, everything in some way relates back to that unified story.
3. Be creative in envisioning and implementing the details. The best historical environments involve some amount of artistry.

## WALT DISNEY, MASTER STORYTELLER

Mention Walt Disney or Disney theme parks to any museum professional and chances are that a negative connotation will emerge.[8] Words like Disneyfication, Disneylandish, and Mickey Mouse history might crop up in the conversation, implying experiences that are contrived, historically inaccurate, and only for entertainment. What we can learn from Walt Disney is not about whether the history is accurate, but how narrative is used to develop park experiences—from lands to attractions to signage, even to trash cans! Like Mary Colter, Walt Disney was a master at transforming stories into three-dimensional environments. But true to his own background, he approached each environment as he would a movie.

Walt Disney, born in 1901, came of age in Missouri—both the small town of Marceline and the urban environment of Kansas City.[9] As a boy, he was enamored with adventure stories and was often found daydreaming in school. He became good friends with another Walt—Walter Pfeiffer, whose family introduced him to the world of theater, vaudeville, and motion pictures. Entering an amateur talent contest with the other Walt, Disney found he could make audiences laugh and began to see himself as an entertainer. Walt Disney also liked to sketch and eventually convinced his austere father (it was actually his mother who did the convincing) to let him attend drawing classes. When he was just twenty-two years old, he and his business-oriented brother Roy moved to Hollywood, where they established an animation studio and started a business from the ground up during the early formative years of this medium.

Walt was always willing to risk everything to try a new technology or a new film format. In 1928, the popularity of his animated character Mickey Mouse made Walt Disney a household name for the first time, and his successes piled up from there. His special talent was taking animated cartoons to a new level by adding story elements that held the interest of and entertained both adults and children. Reaching for the heart and tapping into deeply held and widely shared American values, he seemed to understand instinctively what people wanted to see on screen.

As Walt Disney relates it, his first interest in creating Disneyland dates back to the times he spent watching his daughters ride the carousel at the local park and it occurred to him that "there should be something built, some kind of family park where parents and children could have fun together."[10] Ultimately, the ABC-TV network, anxious to have a weekly Walt Disney series to improve its ratings, agreed to invest in this new kind of park. *Disneyland*, the TV show, premiered October 27, 1954, while the park of the same name opened in Anaheim, California, on July 17, 1955.

Walt Disney brought all the skill and showmanship of his three decades as a filmmaker to every land and attraction in Disneyland. His vision for the park was to have people suspend disbelief and become willing participants in the stories—to actually enter the faraway times and places that had previously only come to life on the screen. Story became the essential organizing principle behind its design, and every element contributed to telling the story. Walt Disney believed that architecture, landscape, characters, food, merchandise, costumes—what today we would call theming—all needed to blend harmoniously in order to further the story.

But in creating Disneyland, Walt Disney also went beyond mere story elements. Telling a good story, to him, involved laying out an entire story sequence. Guests experiencing the lands and attractions at Disneyland would progress through the stories, scene by scene, as if in a movie. A description of how Walt Disney envisioned Main Street, U.S.A., in Disneyland provides a case in point.[11] Loosely inspired by Walt's boyhood recollections of small-town Marceline, Missouri, Main Street, U.S.A., drew upon cherished (and rapidly disappearing) ideals of the 1950s, ideals like community and togetherness (see Figure 2.2). Breaking from the expectation that Disneyland would have multiple entrances like amusement parks of the time, Walt insisted that his park would have only one way in—that took everyone down Main Street. This set the mood and tone for everything else that was to come.

Like the rest of Disneyland, walking down Main Street was intended to feel like entering a movie in which visitors were the actors (see Figure 2.3).

**Figure 2.2.** The shops that make up the streetscape of Disneyland's Main Street, U.S.A. are "cleaned up" versions of the commercial buildings that Walt Disney remembered while growing up in the small town of Marceline, Missouri.
Photo by Caroline Braden

**Figure 2.3. Disneyland guests make their way "through the movie" toward Sleeping Beauty Castle.**
Photo by Caroline Braden

In Walt's parlance, Scene One was the ritual procession under the railroad station, emerging out on the square in front of City Hall. Scene Two was the Plaza, where Main Street almost imperceptibly faded into the central Hub, which gave people a sense of orientation and from which the other lands radiated. Scene Three was the fountain, the statue, and the beckoning Sleeping Beauty Castle. Every part of Main Street—every hitching post, sign, awning, and building cornice—was part of the movie, nothing was there that was not intended. While choices ensued once visitors reached the Hub and headed to different lands, Main Street, U.S.A., was about a single entry point, a setting of the mood, a story unfolding with order and control.

To transform stories into three-dimensional environments, Walt Disney used a few self-selected tools. First, he adapted the use of storyboards from his filmmaking process to the design of each attraction (see chapter 6 for more detail).[12] Second, he felt that architectural drawings did not present the whole story. He insisted on three-dimensional scale models for each land and attraction, to help him visualize relationships, see what worked, and catch incongruities.

One of Walt Disney's most lasting contributions when he created Disneyland was his realization that he could not develop it alone. Using his studio staff as an initial resource, he handpicked a small group of creative artists, animators, and designers from the studio and asked them to dedicate themselves to designing and developing the park with him. Eventually, engineers and technicians were added, forming the group that Walt would call—and are still called—Imagineers.

These veteran storytellers turned ideas (often Walt's) into images and ultimately into the real thing. They had little or no architectural training, but were highly skilled in imagining places where people could participate in an orderly sequence of planned story scenes.[13] Unfortunately, Walt Disney passed away in 1966, only eleven years after Disneyland opened and just as he was beginning to plan what would eventually become (through his brother's efforts) Walt Disney World in Florida. But Walt Disney Imagineering grew in number and skills, and this multitalented group of people has carried on Walt's vision to all Disney parks worldwide.

To aid in the storytelling process, the Imagineers have added a design aid called the "story behind the story" or the "backstory." Written as an outline or narrative, the backstory is the "inside story" that explains the reasoning behind every new experience and plays a key role in defining the details of each project.

What can museum professionals learn from the contributions of Walt Disney and his Imagineers to creating historical environments?

1. "Storyboard" your environment. Most of us aren't artists, but we can envision the sequence and order of an environment—especially one through which visitors walk—by writing a visitor experience walkthrough (see chapter 6).
2. Write a "backstory" for your environment based upon the setting and its real (or representative) inhabitants. Who might have inhabited this space? Why were they here? What were their attitudes, values, aspirations? Then, consider how all your decisions align with your responses to these questions (see chapter 5).
3. Be creative in envisioning and implementing the details. The best environments involve some amount of theatricality and showmanship.

## LIVING HISTORY AND THE "NEW SOCIAL HISTORIANS"

Living history sites are generally considered to be museum-based recreations of historic villages, homes, or farms in which staff members, dressed in period clothing, attempt to simulate life from a certain place and time.[14] Since their inception during the late 1960s and 1970s, these have often fallen under criticism: by academics, for being too simplistic and/or too theatrical; by the public, for being too didactic or too off-putting (especially when using such interpretive techniques as first-person role-playing); and for being difficult to sustain. I would argue that perhaps the most significant and lasting contribution of living history sites to museum practice rarely receives mention—that is, the insistence upon and integration of extensive and rigorous historical research to address both very specific and very broad questions. Over time, these research techniques have come to be considered standard practice for recreating any environment at a historic house, site, or exhibit in which a specific time and place are intended to be portrayed.

Historians of living history generally trace the origin of this approach to open-air museums in Europe, especially the Swedish folk museum Skansen, founded by Artur Hazelius in 1891.[15] But, as Warren Leon and Margaret Piatt claim in their overview of living history museums, American living history sites evolved along a somewhat different path than in Europe—taking more influence from early- and mid-twentieth-century historic houses (often of prominent Americans) and historic preservation efforts (often of a distinguished architecture). The goals of these early efforts were—more or less—to preserve, protect, and glorify what had come to be viewed as traditional American (that is, white Anglo-Saxon Protestant) values against the encroachment of recent European immigration. Historic villages like Colonial Williamsburg (1929), Greenfield Village (1929), Old Sturbridge Village (1946), and Plimoth Plantation (1947) were all founded by wealthy philanthropists as a way to confirm what they perceived were good old American democratic values. By the 1960s, all of these places claimed to show life as lived, in various eras of the past.

Then, in the late 1960s and 1970s, a field emerged in academia called the "new social history."[16] Tracing their discipline's origins to the 1920s-era "Annales School" in France, the new social historians asserted that everyone's history—not just that of the more traditionally studied political, social, and economic elite—was important in understanding historical change through time. These social historians focused new efforts on studying people who lived ordinary lives and did ordinary things—what came to be referred to as "history from the bottom up" or "grassroots history."[17] Although these ordinary people (e.g., working classes, women, enslaved African Americans, impoverished and/or illiterate people, immigrant groups) did not leave much in the public record, the new social historians began to more deeply dig and more imaginatively analyze such sources as census records, diaries, journals, probate and tax records—as well as drawing from the methodologies of such social science disciplines as sociology, anthropology, archaeology, and folklore. Bringing new questions to the analysis of such data, they could draw conclusions about beliefs, customs, and values of individuals, families, and communities as well as about broader societal questions like how people responded to change and disruption.

As it turned out, the new social history showed a remarkable affinity for the settings and subjects that outdoor villages had long depicted. At the same time, these villages also seemed to show a great potential for incorporating larger social history themes. As social historians Barbara and Cary Carson wrote in their article, "Things Unspoken: Learning Social History from Artifacts":

> Births, christenings, schooling, courtship, weddings, housework, farm work, office work, no work, leisure, play, holidays, social gatherings, family reunions, church attendance, sporting events, riots, crimes, broken marriages, illness, deaths, funerals, bereavements—all were acted out in real, three-dimensional settings. All can be vividly recalled—indeed, can only be vividly recalled—when those historical settings are evoked.[18]

A few outdoor museums embraced the precepts of the new social history and set the model for incorporating this methodology into what came to be known as living history—creating a template that numerous others would follow. Among the pioneering champions of this approach were visionaries like anthropologist James Deetz and historian David Freeman at Plimoth Plantation and cultural geographer Darwin Kelsey at Old Sturbridge Village (both sites located in Massachusetts), who brought multidisciplinary scholarship and new interpretive approaches to transform these sites (see Figure 2.4).[19]

Another important reason why the new social historians embraced the notion that outdoor villages could be used as staging grounds for interpreting social history themes was their increased appreciation for the objects that had long made up the decorative assemblages in period rooms.[20] Taking their cue from methodologies developed by archaeologists, the new social historians came to look at these man-made objects—or material culture—as tangible, concrete evidence of past lives and events. They invested ordinary historical artifacts with new meaning, using them to reveal clues about not just everyday life but about such complex ideas as attitudes, values, social conventions, and human relationships.

In a 1984 article entitled, "Old World Wisconsin: What Price Our Heritage?" curator Emilie Tari wrote:

> Material culture is not a discipline, but rather an umbrella concept which can shelter a number of methodologies and a diversity of inquiry. At its heart, however, is the realization that history is also blatantly, persistently, and unarguably three-dimensional.[21]

**Figure 2.4.** This scene of two historically attired interpreters shucking corn at the Pliny Freeman Farm in Old Sturbridge Village, Sturbridge, Massachusetts, reflects an early, groundbreaking integration of social history research with the daily interpretation.
Courtesy Old Sturbridge Village

Following these tenets, Tari created a series of breathtaking room settings at Old World Wisconsin in the late 1970s and early 1980s. These serve as a fitting case study for demonstrating how rigorous new social history methodologies were applied to creating immersive environments at a living history site.

Planning for what would become Old World Wisconsin began in 1968 with a master plan for eighteen ethnic farms that would "show the development and ultimate assimilation of various immigrant populations into 19th-century Wisconsin."[22] At each site, visitors would experience the lives of people from different ethnic groups through interpreters dressed in period clothing, performing daily domestic routines and farming chores.

Researching each farm started by laying out broad historical themes of Wisconsin history and determining which ethnic and immigrant groups best illustrated these. Each group was then researched in detail, using the scant public information that existed from such sources as newspapers, census schedules, and tax records. A prodigious amount of research then went into researching each farm and its structures, including documented sources, archaeological analysis, and material culture study. Old World Wisconsin opened in rural Eagle, Wisconsin, in 1976, administered by the State Historical Society of Wisconsin.

As each structure was chosen to represent a specific place, ethnic group, and family, Tari considered the interior furnishings to be crucial to portraying, as nearly as possible, the individual and idiosyncratic experiences and values of families who had once lived and worked there.[23] She used every available source of evidence to determine the appropriate material culture, not only primary sources that existed like newspapers and census, probate, and tax records, but also oral histories of family and community members; family photo albums and scrapbooks; descriptive accounts of daily life and farming in journals, diaries, and letters; and business records like account books, daybooks, and trade catalogs.

Only after this rigorous scrutiny did Tari begin to determine the appropriate and distinctive furnishings for each structure. For example, after analyzing all the background research she could pull together related to the farm of Norwegian-American Anders Ellingsen Kvaale, she considered each potential artifact and reproduction in relation to three distinct categories: those brought from Norway, those made by immigrants in Wisconsin, and those purchased in Wisconsin. This careful consideration led to subtle differences in material culture between the various families and groups represented at Old World Wisconsin, including slight variations in the same tools and processes. These differences could then be used to both tell specific stories and communicate broader social history themes such as mindset, values, interactions between individuals and community members, and interconnections with the larger world (see Figure 2.5). In her 1984 article, Tari summed up her vision behind these installations:

> Here the three-dimensional world of our forebears can be walked through, touched, experienced in a direct and significant way. Through their things we can learn about them and understand their impact on the past. Historical themes from the intimate fact to the broad generalization divulge new meaning as they are interpreted through those things which people have made and held dear.[24]

What can we take away from the integration of the new social history methodology into early living history sites such as Old World Wisconsin?

1. In doing local history and primary source research, be rigorous and methodical. Leave no stone unturned.
2. Be analytical in finding and assessing sources. What questions are you trying to find answers for? Where might you go to find the answer to these questions? What is this data truly telling you?
3. Ask the big questions. How do minute details lead you to better understand the broader picture about values, mindset, interactions, and interconnections?

**Figure 2.5.** Furnished interior of the Norwegian-American Kvaale family's farmhouse, Old World Wisconsin, Eagle, Wisconsin
Courtesy of Wisconsin Historical Society

## PIONEERING CONTRIBUTIONS:
## DIFFERENCES AND COMMONALITIES

This chapter explored pioneering contributions to historical environments through case studies of architect Mary Colter, master storyteller Walt Disney, and the new social historians who integrated their methodologies into early living history sites. While Mary Colter and Walt Disney were loosely inspired by historical precedents, storytelling was their ultimate aim. In contrast, the primary goal of the new social historians at living history sites was historical accuracy through rigorous research, then integrating this research into interpreting the daily lives of real people living in the past. Each of these pioneering contributors brought their unique background, vision, and approach to creating historical environments. Despite their obvious differences, they also share some—perhaps surprising—commonalities. These include:

- Bringing a unified and coherent vision to defining the environments they created.
- Insisting on a scrupulous attention to detail, which led to having a specific reason for everything and everything in its place.

- Ensuring that the setting was "alive" with the presence of people who had once inhabited it.
- Embracing the role of visitors as active participants in the experience.

Understanding what each of these contributors can teach us, both separately and together, makes our task easier as we begin to actually lay out the steps for creating historical environments in the following chapters.

## NOTES

1. For background on Mary Colter, see Arnold Berke, *Mary Colter: Architect of the Southwest* (New York: Princeton Architectural Press, 2002); and Virginia L. Grattan, *Mary Colter: Builder Upon the Red Earth* (Flagstaff, AZ: Northland Press, 1980).

2. Grattan, *Mary Colter: Builder*, 8.

3. In addition to the above sources, Colter's work at the Grand Canyon is described in Christine Barnes, *Hopi House: Celebrating 100 Years* (Bend, OR: W.W. West, 2005).

4. Berke, *Mary Colter: Architect*, 10.

5. Grattan, *Mary Colter: Builder*, 59–60.

6. Berke, *Mary Colter: Architect*, 93.

7. Grattan, *Mary Colter: Builder*, 59.

8. See, for example, Mike Wallace, "Mickey Mouse History: Portraying the Past at Disney World," in *Mickey Mouse History and Other Essays on American Memory* (Philadelphia, PA: Temple University Press, 1996), 133–58; and paragraph three in William Tramposch, "Mickey and the Muses," *History News* 53, no. 1 (Winter 1998): 10–11.

9. Recommended works on Walt Disney's background and creation of Disneyland include Bob Thomas, *Walt Disney: American Original* (New York: The Walt Disney Company, 1976); Katherine Greene and Richard Greene, *Inside the Dream: The Personal Story of Walt Disney* (New York: Disney Editions, 2001); Brian Burnes, Robert W. Butler, and Dan Viets, *Walt Disney's Missouri: The Roots of a Creative Genius* (Kansas City, MO: Kansas City Star Books, 2002); and Randy Bright, *Disneyland Inside Story* (New York: Henry N. Abrams, Inc., 1987).

10. Quoted in Bright, *Disneyland Inside Story*, 33.

11. For particularly descriptive and enlightening analyses of Main Street, U.S.A. as part of the larger vision of Disneyland, see Karal Ann Marling, "The Place That Was Also a TV Show," chapter 3 in *As Seen on TV: The Visual Culture of Everyday Life in the 1950s* (Cambridge, MA: Harvard University Press, 1994), 86–126; Marling, "Imagineering the Disney Theme Parks," in *Designing Disney's Theme Parks: The Architecture of Reassurance*, ed. Karal Ann Marling (Paris: Flammarion, 1997), 29–177; and Marling, with Donna R. Braden, *Behind the Magic: 50 Years of Disneyland* (Dearborn, MI: The Henry Ford, 2005), 36–49.

12. For more background on Walt Disney's use of storyboards and models in the creation of Disneyland, see The Imagineers, *Walt Disney Imagineering: A Behind the Dreams Look at Making the Magic Real* (New York: Hyperion, 1996), 40–41 and 72–75.

13. For more detail on this process from an early Imagineer who worked directly with Walt Disney on the creation of Disneyland, see John Hench, with Peggy Van Pelt, *Designing Disney: Imagineering and the Art of the Show* (New York: Disney Editions, 2003).

14. Many people have attempted to define living history. See the essay "Living History" on the website for The Association for Living History, Farm and Agricultural Museums (ALHFAM), accessed December 11, 2017, http://www.alhfam.org/living-history-resources. ALHFAM, founded in 1970 at the nascence of the living historical farm movement, is "an international organization for people who bring history to life, open to all people and institutions interested in living historical farms, agricultural museums, and outdoor museums, including but not limited to history, folk life, and agriculture." Accessed December 11, 2017, http://www.alhfam.org/Our-History. Since its inception, this organization has published invaluable proceedings of its annual meetings, many of which are used as reference material here.

15. The evolution of living history museums is detailed in Warren Leon and Margaret Piatt, "Living-History Museums," in *History Museums in the United States: A Critical Assessment*, ed. Warren Leon and Roy Rosenzweig (Urbana, IL: University of Illinois Press, 1989), 64–97.

16. For insightful descriptions and essays on the new social history and its early integration into living history sites, see David E. Kyvig and Myron A. Marty, *Nearby History: Exploring the Past Around You*, 3rd ed. (Lanham, MD: Rowman & Littlefield, 2010), 9–10; Cary Carson, "Living Museums of Everyman's History," in *A Living History Reader*, Vol. 1, *Museums*, ed. Jay Anderson (Nashville, TN: American Association for State and Local History, 1991), 25–31; David G. Vanderstel, "A Behavioral Approach to Living History: The Search for Community in the Past," in *Proceedings of the Annual Meetings in Denver, Colorado, and Williamsburg, Virginia, The Association for Living Historical Farms and Agricultural Museums*, ed. Donna R. Braden, vol. VIII (Washington, DC: Smithsonian Institution, 1988), 76–87; Peter N. Stearns, "The New Social History: An Overview," in *Ordinary People and Everyday Life: Perspectives on New Social History*, ed. James B. Gardner and George Rollie Adams (Nashville, TN: The American Association for State and Local History, 1983), 3–21; and Lynwood Montell, "Social History and Today's Museum," in *Proceedings of the Annual Meeting April 6–9, 1981, Golden Pond and Lake Barkley, Kentucky, The Association for Living Historical Farms and Agricultural Museums* (Washington, DC: Smithsonian Institution, 1983), 6–13.

17. Kyvig and Marty, *Nearby History*, 9.

18. Barbara G. Carson and Cary Carson, "Things Unspoken: Learning Social History from Artifacts," in *Ordinary People*, 182–83.

19. The transformation of Plimoth Plantation and Old Sturbridge Village from outdoor villages to living history sites has been described in numerous articles. Those

related to Plimoth Plantation include Carson, "Living Museums of Everyman's History"; James Deetz, "The Reality of the Pilgrim Fathers," in *A Living History Reader*, 101–109; James W. Baker, "Looking Back—Looking Forward—Looking Around," in *Proceedings of the 1990 Annual Meeting, Providence, Rhode Island*, ed. Debra Reid and Ken Yellis, vol. XIII (Santa Fe, NM: The Association for Living Historical Farms and Agricultural Museums, 1993), 12–18; James Baker, "World View at Plimoth Plantation: History and Theory," in *Proceedings of the 1990 Annual Meeting*, 64–67; and Ken Yellis, "Not Time Machines, But Real Time: Living History at Plimoth Plantation," in *Proceedings of the 1989 Annual Meeting, Indianapolis, Indiana, The Association for Living Historical Farms and Agricultural Museums*, ed. Thomas A. Woods, vol. XII (Santa Fe, NM: Old Cienega Village Museum, 1992), 52–57. Articles related to Darwin Kelsey's establishment of the Pliny Freeman Farm and the beginning of other living history programs at Old Sturbridge Village include Darwin Kelsey, "Harvests of History," in *A Living History Reader*, 69–72; Edward L. Hawes, "The Living History Farm in North America: New Directions for Research and Interpretation," in *A Living History Reader*, 79–97; and Andrew H. Baker and Warren Leon, "Old Sturbridge Village Introduces Social Conflict into Its Interpretive Story," in *A Living History Reader*, 110–118.

    20. Material culture studies applications to living history sites appear in Carson and Carson, "Things Unspoken"; Brooke Hindle, "How Much Is a Piece of the True Cross Worth?" in *Material Culture and the Study of American Life: A Winterthur Book*, ed. Ian M. G. Quimby (New York: W.W. Norton, 1978), 5–20; Carson, "Doing History with Material Culture," in *Material Culture and the Study of American Life*, 41–64; and Deetz, "A Sense of Another World: History Museums and Cultural Change," *Museum News* 58, no. 5 (May/June 1980): 40–45.

    21. Emilie Tari, "Old World Wisconsin: What Price Our Heritage?" *Wisconsin Academy Review* 52 (March 1984): 50.

    22. Leon and Piatt, "Living-History Museums," 79.

    23. Tari's process is detailed in Leon and Piatt, "Living-History Museums," 79; and Betty Kilsdonk, "Is Process Demonstration Historically Credible?" in *Proceedings of the 1987 Annual Meeting, Ann Arbor and Dearborn, Michigan, The Association for Living Historical Farms and Agricultural Museums*, ed. Peter Cousins, vol. X (Washington, DC: Smithsonian Institution, 1989), 20–32.

    24. Tari, "Old World Wisconsin," 50.

# 3

## Framing Your Project

This chapter begins to lay out the process for creating historical environments. Once the decision has been made to begin working on a new exhibition, a historic structure installation, or a historic site upgrade, the excitement is palpable. People want to get started and quickly move forward. But that is not as easy as it sounds. It is inevitable—and human nature—that people working together on a new project will have different ideas and opinions about what it entails and where it is headed. Furthermore, project planning can be complicated and expensive.

The early planning process lays a firm foundation for everything that will follow, ensuring an engaging and effective visitor experience. Early planning will help prevent conflict later; promote team cohesion; help you communicate clearly with staff, stakeholders, and consultants; and save time, money, and resources. It provides a road map to follow and increases the likelihood of the success of your project. Of course, the length, time, and depth of the planning process will differ for every institution and project. The important thing is to engage in a planning process, however it works for you. You can always adjust it as you are going. Remember to write your decisions down. You will find yourself returning to these time and time again.

### HISTORICAL ENVIRONMENTS IN MUSEUM EXHIBITIONS[1]

Historical environments can encompass entire exhibitions, but they usually consist of smaller components, sometimes called vignettes, within a larger exhibition. It is impossible (or at least unwise) to plan a historical environment without first considering the larger exhibition. Next, consider what part this environment plays in the exhibition and how it adds value to the overall visitor experience. The following steps are recommended in planning an environment like this within an exhibition space:

1. Understand the Charge of the Exhibition

   The official project charge might range from an in-depth written "Project Charter" to an informal conversation between director and staff. Knowing the following crucial information up front will have an impact on many later decisions, including the potential for and selection of specific environments:

   • Space and location for exhibition;
   • Size of exhibition;
   • Length of exhibition;
   • Lighting and climate control;
   • Budget;
   • Timetable with opening date and milestone reviews;
   • Resources, including roles and responsibilities of exhibition team members.

2. Establish Institutional Goals

   A list of institutional goals can help clarify expectations for the exhibition project from the senior management level to the exhibition team to the eventual implementers of the program. These goals become the framework for direction and decision-making from an *institutional* (as opposed to a *visitor*) perspective and will have an impact on the environments you create. How does the exhibition relate to your institution's mission, vision, and strategic plan? Why is your museum creating this exhibition? What value does it serve to your museum?

3. Define Target Audiences

   In determining target audiences, aim to reach beyond current museum visitors or the broad general public. Start with what audiences you assume will come to this exhibition, but then consider what new audiences you would like to attract. This list could consider such audiences as the museum's members; specific gender or age groups; hobbyists or enthusiasts of specific topics or collections areas; destination-seeking tourists; informal social groups, such as families or intergenerational groups; and learning-oriented groups, such as camps or after-school clubs. If school-age audiences are to be targeted, be as grade and discipline specific as possible. Consider underserved audiences within your community. Next, learn all you can about the needs, characteristics, and interests of these audiences.[2]

4. Develop a Preliminary Content Framework

Begin to identify major topics, themes, and ideas related to your exhibition (see chapter 4 for more on the research process). What are the accurate, important, and compelling historical stories you want to/should/can tell here? What is your historical point of view, your thesis? How might you divide your essay or content outline into discrete topics? What themes cut across the entire content framework? Turn your research findings into a written report, essay, or content outline. The written piece can vary in length, depending upon the project. Reports might also be written by scholars and other historic advisers that you involve at this point. Also at this time, begin to define the collections you might be using. This is not a final artifact list but an initial understanding of what collections you have (or might need) for your exhibition.

5. Get Outside Input

It is easy to assume that you know what visitors to your museum are thinking. The problem is that we actually often do not know. While we can make educated guesses, visitor knowledge, misperceptions, attitudes, and opinions can surprise even the most knowledgeable among us. One of the best ways to get visitor input at the beginning, middle, and end of an exhibition is through visitor evaluation. Front-end evaluation involves gathering information about visitor knowledge, perceptions, and expectations early in the process.[3] It helps you check how visitors understand a given topic and how this aligns with the expectations of the project team before much money is spent.[4] In doing front-end evaluation, it is important to remember that visitor evaluation involves a rigorous methodology that comes from the discipline of social science. As such, systematic, unbiased testing is very important to the validity of a study. Merely observing visitors in a nonsystematic way can be regarded as "anecdotal" (that is, your own personal opinion) and, as such, considered invalid. You might need to involve evaluation experts in this phase. Be sure to build this into your budget.

This is also a good time to begin to involve community members and advisers to provide input to your project so far.[5] While some might argue that getting this outside input takes time, money, and resources (let alone expertise), it can actually save time and money later as well as help in defining goals, leverage external funding, enhance staff knowledge and cohesion, and increase your local community's interest in your project.

6. Focus the Experience

With your institutional goals, preliminary content framework, potential artifact list, and an initial understanding of visitor knowledge, interests, and expectations in hand, it is time to focus your exhibition. Start by creating one main unifying statement. In the exhibition development world, this is generally referred to as "The Big Idea."[6] According to Beverley Serrell, an expert on developing visitor-focused exhibitions, the Big Idea should be:

- The key idea you want people to know in your exhibition.
- One sentence—and one sentence ONLY!—stating what the exhibition is about. One sentence forces people to focus, and it is much easier to remember than multiple sentences. Often, this sentence includes a subject (topic), an action (what is the subject about?), and a consequence (why should people care?).
- An internal statement that sets the tone, limits the content, and unifies the team vision moving forward. Visitors may never see this statement, or they may see part of it. But when you ask them later what they thought the exhibition was about, their comments should in some way reflect back on this statement. This is very helpful in assessing the success of the exhibition after it is open.
- BIG! It should have fundamental meaningfulness. It should not be trivial.
- Written in concise, everyday language that can be easily understood by internal staff, external design consultants, and stakeholders.

7. Create Visitor-Related Goals

   In exhibition planning, visitor-related exhibition goals have been construed in many ways, such as cognitive/affective goals and knowing/seeing/doing goals. Assuming that the goals for school-age audiences must incorporate specific learning objectives, I like to additionally create what I call visitor experience goals. In determining these, I consider:

- Curiosity—How can we entice visitors to want to know more?
- Personal connection—How can we help visitors feel a kinship with, feel a sense of belonging or connectedness with, and reflect upon their own lives in relation to what we are presenting?
- Social experience—How can we encourage visitors to share thoughts, memories, and feelings with those accompanying them as they experience the exhibition?
- Encounters with objects—How can we further visitors' appreciation of the objects in the exhibition, for their own sake and as they relate to larger themes and stories?

- Connections with people and their stories—How can we encourage visitors to feel empathy for, identify with, respect, or sympathize with the people whose stories are being presented in the exhibition?
- Call to action—How can we inspire visitors to feel energized and empowered by the exhibition so that it has a powerful and lasting impact on their lives?

8. Develop the Preliminary Approach

    At this point, you are ready to begin thinking about your exhibition layout. One of the first decisions you will probably want to make is, should the exhibition be organized chronologically (i.e., progressing through time) or by topic? How does your preliminary content framework inform this decision? Do institutional goals, target audiences, outside input, and visitor-related goals influence this?

9. Finally, the Historical Environment(s)!

    It is around this time that ideas start to emerge about creating environments as a component (or components) within the larger exhibition, and what they might be. Going through a small-scale version of the exhibition planning process can help define the what, the why, and the how of each environment at this point. This includes:

- Describing the environment in a preliminary way.
- Defining the primary message you are trying to get across here: How does it fit your historical thesis, topics, and themes? How does it help accomplish institutional goals? How does it align with visitor-related goals?
- Determining what collections you have (or need) to support this environment.
- Preliminary ideas for the visitor experience: Will visitors look into the space or enter it? What ideas do you have at this point about best communicating the story (interpreters, labels, media)?

The specifics (furnishings plan, interpretive strategy) will be worked out later. This just gets you started. Writing it down will become invaluable as you move forward through the rest of the planning and implementation process.

## CHECKLIST 3.1.
### Written Project Brief for Developing Historical Environments in Exhibitions

A written report at this point is useful for capturing all your thoughts and decisions so far. It should include:

- The charge (including exhibition size and scope, budget, timetable, and resources)
- Institutional goals, including connection to mission
- Target audience(s)
- Preliminary content framework (historical thesis, topics, and themes)
- List of potential collections (haves and needs)
- Findings from community advisers and/or front-end visitor evaluation
- Exhibition Big Idea
- Visitor experience goals and K–12 learning objectives
- Preliminary approach
- The historical environment(s)

  ○ Description
  ○ Primary message
  ○ Potential collections (haves and needs)
  ○ Preliminary experience ideas

## REAL-LIFE EXAMPLE: "BACK-TO-THE-LAND" COMMUNE, *YOUR PLACE IN TIME: 20TH CENTURY AMERICA* EXHIBITION[7]

### Project Charge, Institutional Goals, and Target Audience

The creation of this environment started with the charge to an internal project team to develop an exhibition that would be the Museum's "statement on the 20th century."

Further information gathering from senior-level staff revealed that it should focus upon the impact of technology on people's lives during the twentieth century. Other institutional goals for the exhibition included:

- Refining a model for exhibition development in which the exhibition was more experience driven than collections or content driven.
- Representing diverse groups in the personal stories told in the exhibition.
- Providing opportunities and settings that would encourage intergenerational learning and sharing.

Target audiences determined at this time included:

- The Museum's daily visitors.
- Underserved audiences (especially diverse local communities).
- Nonmuseum audiences (for a traveling component of the exhibition created in collaboration with *Popular Mechanics* magazine).
- School-age audiences (specific grades and subjects were to be determined at this time).

## Preliminary Content Framework

Project team members began researching the topic of the changing relationship between people and technology during the twentieth century. Fairly early on, team members found that an important key to this was that the specific generation in which people came of age played a major role in this relationship. The thesis of the exhibition ultimately came to embody the idea that certain personal experiences—conditioned by and connected with different technologies—helped define each new generation of the twentieth century. An important point in the content framework, as it related to the eventual creation of the "Back-to-the-Land" Commune environment, was that the team wanted to encourage visitors to consider both the positive and negative aspects of twentieth-century technologies as they encountered specific experiences and attitudes of each generation.

## Visitor Input and Big Idea

During the planning stage, the exhibition team conducted extensive front-end audience evaluation, including surveys and interviews. An important study was to determine what basic exhibit concept (out of four the team had developed) might most appeal to our visitors. Of 100 surveys completed, the top choice was the generations approach (described in the survey as "looking at how our outlooks and attitudes are based, in part, on what years we grew up in"). This led to the exhibition's Big Idea:

> This exhibit invites you to explore the rich interplay between people and technology by looking at the five generations who came of age in the 20th century.

**Figure 3.1.** Entrance to the *Your Place in Time: 20th Century America* exhibition, Henry Ford Museum of American Innovation
Photo by Deborah Berk

## Visitor Experience Goals

Building upon the planning process thus far, the visitor experience goals incorporated both cognitive and affective aspects to reinforce personal meaning-making and the social experience and to include a longer-term impact or "call to action." These goals included:

- Inspiring curiosity, wonder, and a sense of recognition as visitors "see themselves" and others in this exhibit.
- Evaluating their own past (and that of others) and how their life experiences have been connected to and shaped by technology.
- Seeing and understanding how earlier technologies have evolved and still influence the technologies they use today.
- Assessing how technology has influenced their lifestyle choices and how their choices have influenced technology.
- Imagining and speculating what the future might hold and how they and the next generations will respond to and shape present and future technologies.

## Preliminary Approach

With the generations approach determined and an institutional goal of "re-fining a model for exhibition development in which the exhibition is more experience-driven than collections- or content-driven," a major portion of the exhibition became a series of "Generations Experiences." This involved, for each generation who came of age during the twentieth century, a series of richly textured historical environments—that is, themed vignettes and/or interactive spaces that contained varied combinations of artifacts, large wall murals, graphics, audio, video, and hands-on activities. The team adopted the idea of Visitor Panels from the field of visitor studies as a way to gain access to a range of stories for the "Generations Experiences" from groups of people with diverse life experiences.[8] Additionally, this ensured that the "right" stories for each generation were chosen as exhibition experiences. The Visitor Panels, made up of five to eight people, met several times and helped to inform the final choices of experiences.

## Planning for the "Back-to-the-Land" Commune Environment

After the "Generations Experiences" approach was determined, project team members returned to the existing scholarship, delving more deeply into the characteristics of the five generations who came of age during the twentieth century and their specific interaction with technology. Brief written reports of their findings summarized these characteristics and included suggestions of possible exhibition experiences related to them. These eventually led to a main message for each generation and, through evolving team discussions, to the final choices of experiences. The main message for the section on the Baby Boomer generation read:

> With their large numbers and vast buying power, members of this generation constituted their own market for new, ever-changing products and technologies geared especially to them. At the same time, a portion of the youth of this generation grew increasingly skeptical and distrustful of "Big Technologies," controlled by the government, the military, and big business.

Ensuing discussions of how to convey negative attitudes toward these "Big Technologies" ultimately led to the idea of creating an environment (inside a geodesic dome) that would represent "back-to-the-land" communal living.

**Figure 3.2.**   Baby Boomer section of the *Your Place in Time: 20th Century America* exhibition, with the 1973 "Back-to-the-Land" Commune environment in the background, Henry Ford Museum of American Innovation
Courtesy of The Henry Ford

## ENVIRONMENTS IN HISTORIC STRUCTURES

Though there are exceptions, planning an environment within a historic structure or an entire historic site generally comes much earlier in the process than in exhibition planning. This is because the environment is an essential component of—if not one and the same as—that structure or the structures that make up that site. Creating a historical environment in these contexts generally falls under the heading of interpretive planning.

In her essay, "Interpretation Planning: Why and How," Barbara Abramoff Levy explains that an interpretive plan is "meant to guide the site in determining what meanings and relationships it wants to reveal as well as how, and for whom it should do this."[9] The following steps are recommended for creating environments within historic structures or sites:

1. Understand the Charge

    This is a description of the task at hand, which—like the exhibition plan—includes budget, timetable, and resources. It additionally might involve a historic structure report, an archaeological findings report, an interpretive master plan, and/or a historic preservation plan.

2. Establish Institutional Goals

   Like exhibition planning, the reason for engaging in an interpretive planning or reinstallation project should be closely related to your museum's mission, vision, and strategic plan. What needs does the plan address? Is it related to preservation goals, ADA compliance, new interpretive priorities, and/or new audience goals? Are there existing reports (for example, a historic structure report, interpretive master plan, research report, collections inventory, or funding proposal) that describe these goals already and can help in determining how to proceed?

3. Define Target Audiences

   This list will generally involve current visitors to the structure or site, but attention should be paid to whether there are underserved audiences or specific new audiences your museum would like to or can attract through this new experience. Determining these at this stage may shift the approach you take for your historical environment(s).

4. Develop a Preliminary Content Framework

   Like the exhibition plan, this involves historical research (see chapter 4 for more on the research process). Like exhibition planning, this step might require the involvement of scholars and other historic advisers. Usually, because the site or structure is a known entity, this will involve local history research in primary documents. This step will generally result in a determination of the most advantageous time and place for its interpretation. It might end up becoming the era of best documented research or address an institutional goal that leads the planning in a somewhat different direction.[10] This is also a good time to start assessing collections strengths and weaknesses. A more in-depth study of this will come later.

5. Get Outside Input

   Implementing front-end visitor evaluation and/or engaging community members at this phase can help you in terms of the topics you interpret and how you interpret them (see earlier description of front-end evaluation in the "Historical Environments in Museum Exhibitions" section).[11] Topics deemed potentially controversial at this early stage can help staff members be better prepared in furnishing the space and interpreting it to the public.

6. Create Visitor Experience Goals

   Interpretive planners often use the term "visitor outcomes" to establish specific visitor-focused goals for a historic structure or site. These should ideally be aimed at "provoking in audiences the discovery of personal meanings and the forging of personal connections."[12] See the "Create Visitor Experience Goals" in the "Historical Environments in Museum Exhibitions" section for points to consider when creating visitor-focused goals. How can visitors personally connect with the people, the place, the events, and the activities that took place here in the past? Determining this now will help you later.

7. Focus the Experience

Instead of the term "Big Idea" commonly used in exhibition planning, interpretive planners often use the term "Main, or Primary, Message." These both imply basically the same thing—determining the broadest and most significant idea that will serve as an umbrella for smaller, interrelated ideas. Together, these form a hierarchy of ideas, which interpretive planners often refer to as "thematic interpretation."[13]

In planning this thematic interpretation, the Main, or Primary, Message should be followed by a series of themes. While these vary among different interpretive planners, I find that three interpretive themes present a nice symmetry. These become the key ideas that will both guide you through the planning process and help visitors later get a focused understanding of what is most unique or significant about your site or structure. According to Levy, each of these themes should

- present one discrete idea;
- be specific enough to have focus but not be too narrow;
- give unity and coherence to multiple things;
- serve as a "basket" for other smaller concepts;
- and be inherent in, illustrated by, or supportive of the material culture and physical evidence at the site.

8. Develop the Preliminary Approach

At this point, you are ready to begin thinking about the actual experience of your historical environment. How literal will you be in recreating time and place? Questions of heat, air-conditioning, light, and accessibility needs should be considered at this time, for both visitor comfort and long-term sustainability of the artifacts. Will real artifacts be used? Will they be accessible to visitors? Will you be encouraging visitors to touch things? Should you consider reproductions? What form of interpretation might this experience take (for example, a guided tour, stationed interpreters, or written interpretive panels to aid visitors in a self-guided experience)? What additional interpretive techniques might you incorporate (for example, an app tour, audio, flipbook, touchable elements)? How do existing planning reports inform the interpretation this setting might eventually take? How do goals, target audiences, visitor input, messages, and existing reports inform possible interpretive strategies? This is only the beginning of your exploration into these questions. You will continue to hone your thinking about them as you move forward.

**CHECKLIST 3.2.**
**Written Project Brief for Developing Environments in Historic Structures**

A written report is useful at this point to document all your thoughts and decisions so far about the historical environment you will be creating. It should include:

- The charge (including budget, timetable, and resources)
- Summary of previous reports that help inform this plan
- Institutional goals for the environment, including relation to mission
- Target audience(s)
- Preliminary research report to determine time and place of the environment
- List of potential collections (haves and needs) for use in the environment
- Findings from community members and/or front-end visitor evaluation
- Main message for the environment
- Interpretive themes (3) for the environment
- Visitor outcomes for the environment
- Preliminary approach to the environment
- Implementation plan

## REAL-LIFE EXAMPLE: REINSTALLATION OF J. R. JONES GENERAL STORE[14]

### Project Charge, Institutional Goals, and Target Audiences

As part of a long-range plan to restore and reinstall several buildings in Greenfield Village, a project team was appointed to research, restore, reinstall, and reinterpret the historic general store. This high-visibility structure on the Village Green had physical integrity, but the interpretation was confusing. The building came from the rural village of Waterford, Michigan, while the Elias Brown store sign out front came from upstate New York. Furthermore, the store stock represented a span of several decades. These inconsistencies led to a generic interpretation of this structure as a "typical," "old-timey" general store, with interpreters often referencing the general stores of pioneer days or Oleson's Mercantile from the *Little House on the Prairie* TV show (see Figure 3.4).

In addition to interpreting a more cohesive, mission-focused story, other institutional goals included:

- Assessing preservation needs of this building and its collections.
- Documenting the building's extensive collections (both on display and on numerous shelves in a second-floor storage space).
- Adding an ADA-compliant ramp for access to the building.

Figure 3.3. Members of the Lah-de-Dahs vintage baseball team pose in front of the newly reinstalled J. R. Jones General Store, 1994, Greenfield Village, Dearborn, Michigan. This team was formed after 1880s newspapers revealed that Waterford, Michigan, boasted a baseball club of that name.

**Figure 3.4.** "Old-timey" interior of the J. R. Jones General Store in Greenfield Village when it was called the Elias Brown General Store, 1965
Courtesy of The Henry Ford

Target audiences included:

- Daily visitors to Greenfield Village.
- Visitors to changing seasonal events and programs.
- School-age audiences, especially focusing upon the subjects of Michigan history and economics.
- Teachers pursuing professional development opportunities.

**Preliminary Content Framework**

As a result of several research projects (including local history, general store history, a study of general store daybooks, a collections documentation project, and a conservation survey), the project team recommended that the restoration, reinstallation, and daily program focus upon the role of this store within the community of Waterford, Michigan, between 1882 and 1888. Research revealed that the storekeepers of this building had changed hands approximately nine times between the 1850s and 1927, when Henry Ford brought it to Greenfield Village. Of its many storekeepers, the best documented one was James R. Jones, who ran the store from 1882 to 1888. The scope of the existing general store collections supported the decision to interpret the installation during the 1880s, as did the fact that this decade was a pivotal period in the changing patterns of rural consumerism, which connected to mission and provided the best opportunities for interpretation. See the research methodology for this project in chapter 4 for more detail.

### Visitor Input, Main Message, and Interpretive Themes

In a front-end evaluation, visitors were asked to choose their three favorite choices of topics from seven that were listed and to rank them first, second, and third. The top choice was "what customers purchased and what their lives were like." Second was "learning more about the merchandise on display." The lowest ranked topics were "how this General Store ended up in Greenfield Village" and "the business of storekeeping."[15] From this input, we gave the customers a major focus in our Main Message:

> The J. R. Jones General Store will combine people, issues, and objects, to show that making purchasing choices in the 1880s was as complicated as it is today, involving people's background, lifestyles, and personal values.

Over time, this message proved to be both too ambitious and too abstract. We revised it to focus upon what visitors immediately encounter when they enter the space and how these encounters can serve as jumping-off points to tell a larger, more complex history:

> The J. R. Jones General Store provides a unique window into people's daily lives in the village of Waterford, Michigan, during the 1880s—an era of rapid change in America.[16]

All of the stories told through this "unique window" would involve a continual interconnection between storekeeping, customers, and products. This led to the following three interpretive themes related to the store:

- Storekeeper J. R. Jones demonstrated a great deal of ingenuity in trying to attract customers to the store.

- Customers were resourceful in their purchasing choices, involving their backgrounds, economic and social standing, and personal values.
- A ready availability of goods from national and international markets at this point in time represented not only an increase in the number and variety of available products but also the beginning of a shift from generic bulk goods to individually packaged, brand-name products.

## Visitor Outcomes

Aligning with the structure's Main Message and interpretive themes, the visitor outcomes became:

As a result of the interaction with setting, objects, and people, visitors to the J. R. Jones General Store will:

- Become impressed by the quantity, variety, and far-reaching origins of products.
- Be curious about what the products are and how they fit into people's daily lives.
- Learn respect for the risks and choices of sellers and buyers at this time.
- Feel a kinship with the original customers to this store, realizing that the process of making decisions about purchases is similar in many respects to the ways in which we make decisions today.

## Preliminary Approach to the J. R. Jones Store

To truly recreate the historic environment of a general store interior from the 1880s, it became crucial to think about the store and its stock and setting as a "working store" environment. This implied that it would be organized into discreet "departments," like historic general stores, and that it would need to include quantities of similar objects that looked as new and unused as possible. Such additions as advertisements, community notices, and an office area for J. R. Jones would help to further communicate the interconnections between storekeeping, customers, and products. Moving forward, there was much work to be done!

## NOTES

1. This section draws from the following published articles and unpublished conference presentations by Donna R. Braden: "Your Personal Toolkit: Easing through Friction, Fracas, and Free-for-All," *N.A.M.E. Exhibitionist* 29, no. 1 (Spring 2010): 6–14; "Taste-Testing the Visitor Experience," *Proceedings of the 2013 Conference*

*and Annual Meeting, Hale Farm & Village, Akron, Ohio*, ed. Debra A. Reid, vol. XXXVI (North Bloomfield, OH: The Association for Living History, Farm and Agricultural Museums, 2014): 197–211; "Great Exhibits Don't Happen by Accident" (paper presented with Dean Krimmel at the 2015 American Association for State and Local History Annual Meeting, Louisville, KY, September 19, 2015); "Where to Begin? The First Steps of Exhibition Planning" (workshop presented at the 2016 Association of Midwest Museums Annual Conference and Meeting, Minneapolis, MN, July 27, 2016); "What Are They Thinking? Visitor-Centered Exhibition Planning" (paper presented with Lorrie Beaumont and Sheila Brommel at the 2016 Association of Midwest Museums Annual Conference and Meeting, Minneapolis, MN, July 27, 2016); and "Rowing in the Same Direction: Building Collaborative Project Teams" (paper presented with Cynthia Torp at the 2017 Association of Midwest Museums Annual Conference and Meeting, Des Moines, IA, July 15, 2017).

2. Learning about audiences can be approached from many different perspectives, including background/heritage, age/life cycle stage, generation, gender, lifestyle, and identity. I recommend starting with three foundational publications by John H. Falk and Lynn D. Dierking, *The Museum Experience* (Washington, DC: Whalesback Books, 1992); *Learning from Museums: Visitor Experiences and the Making of Meaning* (Walnut Creek, CA: AltaMira Press, 2000); and *Lessons without Limit: How Free-Choice Learning Is Transforming Education* (Walnut Creek, CA: AltaMira Press, 2002). Helpful in-depth studies of specific museum audiences include Susie Wilkening and James Chung, *Life Stages of the Museum Visitor: Building Engagement over a Lifetime* (Washington, DC: The AAM Press, 2009); *Connecting Kids to History with Museum Exhibitions*, ed. D. Lynn McRainey and John Russick (Walnut Creek, CA, 2010); "Enriching the Visitor Experience for Kids and Families," entire issue of *N.A.M.E. Exhibitionist* 27, no. 1 (Spring 2008); Lynn D. Dierking, Jessica J. Luke, Kathryn A. Foat, and Leslie Adelman, "The Family and Free-Choice Learning," *Museum News* 80, no. 6 (November/December 2001): 38–43+; Aleah Vinick and Rachel Abbott, "How to Design Programs for Millennials," *History News* 70, no. 4 (Autumn 2015): Technical Leaflet #272; and John H. Falk, *Leisure Decisions Influencing African American Uses of Museums* (Washington, DC: American Association of Museums, 1993). Many audience studies undertaken at individual institutions can be found online.

3. Helpful published works on front-end evaluation include *Introduction to Museum Evaluation*, ed. Minda Borun and Randi Korn (Washington, DC: American Association of Museums, 1999); Jill Stein, Marianna Adams, and Jessica Luke, "Thinking Evaluatively: A Practical Guide to Integrating the Visitor Voice," *History News* 62, no. 2 (Spring 2007): Technical Leaflet #238; Lynn D. Dierking, Robert Kihne, Ann Grimes Rand, and Marilyn Solvay, "Laughing and Learning Together: Family Learning Research Becomes Practice at the U.S.S. Constitution Museum," *History News* 61, no. 3 (Summer 2006): 12–15; and Stacy Klingler and Conny Graft, "In Lieu of Mind Reading: Visitor Studies and Evaluation," in *The Small Museum Toolkit, Book 4: Reaching and Responding to the Audience*, ed. Cinnamon Catlin-Legutko and Stacy Klingler (Lanham, MD: AltaMira Press, a Division of Rowman & Littlefield, 2012), 37–74.

4. Keep in mind that front-end evaluation is just one of many tools at your disposal as you consider your direction. The goal is not to slavishly follow the findings of a visitor study but to simply become aware of visitor perceptions at this early stage.

5. See chapter 7 for two examples in which community engagement was part of the planning process for historical environments: Minnesota History Center's *Open House: If Walls Could Talk* and the Heart Mountain Interpretive Center. See also Jane Mitchell Eliasof, "The Many Voices of a Historic House," *History News* 72, no. 1 (Winter 2017): 14–18; and the section on "Relationship Building" in the "National Summit on Teaching Slavery" report, 2018, James Madison's Montpelier website, accessed January 24, 2019, https://www.montpelier.org/learn/tackling-difficult-history. There are many published works that describe the rationale for, and include relevant case studies related to, involving communities in museum exhibition and program planning, including Barbara B. Walden, "Like a Good Neighbor: Community Advocacy for Small Museums," in *The Small Museum Toolkit, Book 4: Reaching and Responding to the Audience*, ed. Cinnamon Catlin-Legutko and Stacy Klingler (Lanham, MD: AltaMira Press, a Division of Rowman & Littlefield, 2012), 79–97; and Candace Tangorra Matelic, "New Roles for Small Museums, in *The Small Museum Toolkit, Book 4*, 141–162. For a helpful overview on how to create community engagement dialogues and workshops, see *Civic Engagement: A Challenge to Museums* and its companion publication, *A Museum and Community Toolkit* (Washington, DC: American Association of Museums, 2002).

6. See chapter 1, "Behind It All: The Big Idea," in Beverly Serrell's *Exhibit Labels: An Interpretive Approach*, 2nd ed. (Lanham, MD: Rowman & Littlefield, 2015), 7–18.

7. This case study draws from two unpublished manuscripts: "The 20th Century Exhibit Project Plan" (9 November 1998); and Implementation Grant Proposal to the National Endowment for the Humanities for the *Your Place in Time: 20th Century America* Exhibition (29 January 1999), Donna Braden Papers, Benson Ford Research Center, The Henry Ford, Dearborn, MI (hereafter cited as Braden Papers).

8. For more on this topic, see Daryl K. Fischer, "Connecting with Visitor Panels," *Museum News* 76, no. 3 (May/June 1997): 33–37.

9. Barbara Abramoff Levy, "Interpretation Planning: Why and How," in *Interpreting Historic House Museums*, ed. Jessica Foy Donnelly (Lanham, MD: AltaMira Press, a Division of Rowman & Littlefield, 2002), 43. Another invaluable interpretive planning tool, prepared by the National Park Service, is available online at https://www.nps.gov/subjects/hfc/upload/interp-visitor-exper.pdf. Additional books and articles devoted to the topic of interpretive planning include Freeman Tilden's seminal 1957 work that resulted from a commission by the National Park Service, *Interpreting Our Heritage*, 2nd ed. (Chapel Hill: University of North Carolina Press, 1967); Lisa Brochu and Tim Merriman, *Personal Interpretation: Connecting Your Audience with Heritage Resources*, 2nd ed. (Fort Collins, CO: National Association for Interpretation, 2008); Michael P. Gross and Ron Zimmerman, "Park and Museum Interpretation: Helping Visitors Find Meaning," *Curator: The Museum Journal* 45, no. 4 (October 2002): 265–76; Sam H. Ham, *Environmental Interpretation: A Practical Guide for People with Big Ideas and Small Budgets* (Golden, CO: Fulcrum

Publishing, 1993) and *Interpretation: Making a Difference on Purpose* (Golden, CO: Fulcrum Publishing, 2013); John A. Veverka, *Interpretive Master Planning*, Vol. 1, *Strategies for the New Millennium* (Edinburgh: MuseumsEtc, 2011) and *Interpretive Master Planning*, Vol. 2, *Selected Essays: Philosophy, Theory, Practice* (Edinburgh: MuseumsEtc, 2011).

10. If your site or structure is already listed in the National Register of Historic Places, a record will already be on file of its historical significance, based upon the historical context of an event, a person, distinctive physical characteristics, or its potential to yield important information. This already existing assessment points to a likely time and place for its interpretation. For more about the National Register of Historic Places, see https://www.nps.gov/nr/.

11. See note 5 on community engagement examples and strategies.

12. Ham, *Interpretation*, 8.

13. For more on this, see Ham, *Environmental Interpretation*, 33–40; and Levy, "Interpretation Planning," 51–53.

14. This case study draws from Donna R. Braden, "The Process and the Product: Transforming the General Store in Greenfield Village," *History News* 50, no. 3 (Summer 1995): 20–24; Donna R. Braden and Mary Lynn Heininger, "General Stores: The Process and the Product," *Proceedings of the 1993 Conference and Annual Meeting, St. Paul, Minnesota*, ed. Mary Seelhorst and Susan Gangwere McCabe, Vol. XVI (Santa Fe, NM: The Association for Living Historical Farms and Agricultural Museums, 1994), 42–70; and two unpublished reports: "General Store Project Plan" (9 September 1991); and "General Store Project Proposal Restatement/Program Brief" (29 May 1992), Braden Papers.

15. Keep in mind that sometimes the phrasing of a survey question may be leading. While "the business of storekeeping" ranked low in the survey, it turned out that visitors are actually curious about and actually have numerous questions about this topic, but this phrasing likely made the topic sound overly didactic. A pretest of survey questions with a few visitors is always desirable so that questions can be reworded before too many surveys have been completed.

16. "J. R. Jones General Store Training Manual" (unpublished manuscript, March 2017), Braden Papers.

# 4

## Your Research Methodology

Several times in the process of creating an exhibition vignette or historic structure installation, you will be engaging in historical research. Developing a historical environment "based on a rigorous examination of available sources" is what separates best practice in a museum from environments created for theme parks and commercial venues.[1] This process also helps prevent an almost natural inclination to base decisions on personal taste and/or purely aesthetic preferences.

### GETTING STARTED

Where do you begin? Whether you are in the preliminary content framework phase or engaging later in a deeper dive into the topic, a solid research methodology uses what historians call the historical method. According to the authors of *Introduction to Public History: Interpreting the Past, Engaging Audiences*, this involves:

> the systematic and critical examination of sources within their historical contexts to reveal stories of the past, to explain change and continuity over time, to consider contingency, and to reconcile competing versions of past events as preserved in a variety of historical sources.[2]

To begin this examination, it is best to start with a question or series of questions. As historian Jennifer Ford wrote in the article, "Chinking Between the Logs: Reinterpreting the Miller House at Meadowcroft Museum of Rural Life" (a project described later in this chapter):

If as a researcher you approach your source material without questions to ask, mysteries to solve, or hypotheses to test you will end up with bushels of interesting trivia. If however you approach your data with issues to address, when you read through inventories and ledgers and diaries and newspapers you will be alert to clues. When clues string together they form patterns and when you begin to see patterns you are on your way to answering your original questions. When you find answers to questions then you are in a position to explain local history to your visitors rather than just sharing interesting trivia with them.[3]

This process of historical inquiry helps you determine what you want to know and where to begin looking for the answers. Chances are that, throughout the course of your research, you will move from specifics to broader context and from broader context back to specifics. The authors of the invaluable book, *Nearby History: Exploring the Past Around You*, suggest a series of questions relating to the specifics of time, place, and people.[4] As for broader context, historians' search for answers often falls into recognizable patterns: cause and effect, change and continuity, historical turning points, using the past to seek guidance about current problems, and "trying to imagine the world through the eyes of people from different times, places, and conditions to examine the ways in which they made sense of their world."[5] Do not be surprised if new questions continue to arise. These offer renewed chances to unearth the mysteries of the past and add pieces to the jigsaw puzzle you are trying to assemble.

After determining the questions for which you are seeking answers, you can begin to identify research sources. Historians aim for a wide range of materials, using these to form a coherent argument that helps address their questions as well as providing broader meaning and significance to past events. When do you know that you have looked at enough sources? When—and only when— you feel that you are no longer finding anything to add to your puzzle.

In your search for answers, each source will uncover bits of data that will reveal new insight. Sometimes, sources will conflict. In this case, you will have to evaluate each one and decide which is most valid. Historians are so used to doing this that it is almost second nature to them. To help beginning researchers work through this, it is useful to develop a "sourcing heuristic"— that is, a series of steps that historians walk through before analyzing the content of a document.[6] Addressing certain questions about the source's strengths and weaknesses provides a road map for weighing the evidence revealed by each source and helping to establish its authenticity, credibility, accuracy, and usefulness. These questions can include:

- When, where, and how was it created?
- How was it used at the time of creation?

- What kind of evidence does it offer?
- What are its strengths and advantages?
- What are its limitations and biases?[7]

Bringing a healthy skepticism to assessing each bit of evidence is a good habit to adopt. The more sources you find in agreement, the more you can trust them and move toward closure in assembling your puzzle. It is important to remember that it is impossible to ever know what actually happened in the past. So you must make a best guess based upon what seems most probable by weighing all the evidence. This is why going to a wide range of sources is desirable. See Table 4.1 for a list of sources with major pros and cons.

**Table 4.1.  Types of Research Sources with Major Pros and Cons**

| Source | Pros | Cons |
|---|---|---|
| Secondary | Convenient | Dependent upon author's interpretation of information |
| Primary— Published | Original intent of wide distribution makes these easy to find and often quite in-depth | Original purpose for their publication contains potential bias |
| Primary— Unpublished | These date to actual time being studied | Contain bits of data that may conflict and/or not add up |
| Visual | Provide rich pictorial representations | May have been manipulated |
| Oral History | High level of detail and emotion | Likely contain factual errors because based upon memory |
| Material Culture Evidence | Offers concrete evidence of past time, place, people, and mindset | Needs expertise to understand how to interpret |
| Structure | Offers concrete evidence of past time, place, people, and mindset | Good chance of change over time, which requires expertise to interpret |

While there is some overlap, sources can vary widely by the time, place, and type of environment you are researching. Get to know the sources for your specific place, time period, and purpose. Locate and check out other research projects with similar questions. Master's theses, dissertations, and other museums' projects are especially useful in this regard. One source may lead you to another, through its footnotes and/or bibliography. Be strategic as you search for answers to your research questions; be creative in identifying new sources to uncover; and be critical as you sift and sort, evaluate, and analyze until you feel satisfied with your findings. Finally, be open to asking new questions, then delving once again into available research sources.

A word of warning must be given about doing historical research on the Internet.[8] The increasing plethora of material on the Internet has facilitated the search for information of all types. Digitized materials from libraries, archives, and other repositories have made possible easy access to a vast array of distant, hard-to-find, or previously inaccessible material, including historical journals, government documents, genealogical materials, newspapers, magazines, books, and images. This is, for the most part, a wonderful boon to researchers. But one must proceed with extreme caution through this material. There are no universally accepted standards for placing documents and other materials on the Web. Lacking context or provenance, many documents can be misleading, inaccurate, impossible to identify or date, or totally fabricated. It is important to know exactly what the document is, where it came from, and whether it is a reliable source. Also keep in mind that, at least at this point, documents accessible on the Web still only present a fraction of all the material available in archives, county courthouses, universities, public libraries, and elsewhere.

## SECONDARY SOURCES

### Published Books and Articles

It is a comfort, particularly to beginning researchers, to know that—sometime, somewhere—something was probably written about the topic you are researching. New research often begins with secondary sources—that is, published books and articles that analyze the past from a later time in an attempt to synthesize, provide perspective to, or make sense of that place and time. Surveying the secondary literature on a topic is often the most straightforward way to start and involves the easiest sources to track down. But, while convenient to access, these sources are fraught with research problems. When was the source written? What are the author's credentials? What is his or her point of view? Did the author use sources taken directly from the era? How are these interpreted? Are the author's claims footnoted?[9] A good research methodology for a museum's historical environment will usually incorporate secondary sources but will need other kinds of sources as well, to validate, reinforce, and confirm those sources and to provide greater specificity and detail.

### Graduate Theses and Dissertations

These can be incredibly valuable and insightful sources of information, often involving the collecting and analyzing of primary sources with attempts to piece together a bigger picture and reach broad conclusions. Many of these explore aspects of local history at specific places and times. The main drawback of these sources is that their authors tended to create them early in their careers, exploring new, unfamiliar topics and perhaps even using unfamiliar sources and methodology. In fact, the purpose of these is often to gain familiarity with methodologies like using primary sources, synthesizing information, and drawing larger conclusions. Since 1938, dissertations have been available on microfilm at University Microfilms International in Ann Arbor, Michigan, and are indexed on Dissertation Abstracts International. Full-text access to graduate theses and dissertations is now available online through PQDT [ProQuest Dissertations and Theses] Global.

## PRIMARY SOURCES[10]

Primary sources are "documents, images, or artifacts that provide firsthand testimony or direct evidence concerning an historical topic under research investigation."[11] This myriad group of sources—created during or around the time period being studied—is usually harder to access, both physically and conceptually, than secondary sources. But familiarizing yourself with the range of primary sources that is available for the time, place, and situation you are researching can open up a vast world of opportunity for telling richer and deeper stories in your historical environment. Keep in mind that each primary source will usually reveal only small bits of data. These need to be collected and compared with each other, with other primary sources, and with other types of sources, to build a more complete picture. It may seem frustrating at first to find little fragments that do not seem to add up to much, but every bit of data contributes a potentially crucial piece to the larger jigsaw puzzle you are assembling.

Because they were created at or near the time period being studied, primary sources give the impression of being accurate. But, like secondary sources, they can also contain biases. Primary sources were intended for many different purposes, almost none of which were to use as later historical documents! They can be inaccurate, muddled, hearsay, or intended to persuade or mislead. Some were intended for personal use, whereas others were created for strictly documentary purposes—and even then filled with misinformation. One must constantly assess the origin of the source, evaluate its worth and accuracy, and compare it with other sources.

### Published Primary Documents

Published primary documents are sources of which multiple copies were printed for wide dissemination. These include:

- Period literature like advice books, etiquette books, home furnishings books, how-to books, and cookbooks.
- Published journals, diaries, memoirs, biographies, and travel accounts.
- City and county directories and gazetteers, generally published annually with listings of local residents and often including their occupations.
- Periodicals and/or magazines of the period, useful for both articles and advertisements.
- Newspapers of the period, for articles, advertisements, community news, and obituaries (see Figure 4.1).
- County atlases: Many of these bound collections of maps and supplementary local information were published around the time of America's Centennial celebration in 1876, then again in the early twentieth century.
- City and county histories, published during similar eras as county atlases.
- Published business histories.
- Ephemera, including booklets, pamphlets, and programs.
- Government reports.
- Trade literature, including trade catalogs and mail-order catalogs.

**Figure 4.1.** When newspaper advertisements mentioned that a farmer named Richard King produced and sold Westchester Pickles in Waterford, Michigan, during the 1880s, stenciling his name and the name of his pickles on reproduction barrels helped reinforce the immersive quality and sense of place at the J. R. Jones General Store.
Photo by Deborah Berk

These types of sources are increasingly available in digitized form (for example, on Google Books) or listed in online databases or indexes, though you should never assume that if you cannot find it on the Internet it does not exist. It is always best to check with the libraries, museums, and other repositories in the local area you are researching. A check on the websites of, and/or contacting the staff that work at, those local repositories might reveal a description or finding aid that leads you to an invaluable document or collection in their holdings.

Published primary documents can be extremely useful links to the past, as they were produced for wide distribution at the time. But they must also be evaluated for bias. What is the context? Who created it? What was the author's intent in creating it? What was his or her motivation and point of view? For example, published biographies and memoirs were often skewed to present the person in a positive light. Newspapers were often slanted toward a particular political party as well as being produced so hurriedly that they often omitted or distorted facts. Period advice, etiquette, and furnishings books were all intended to persuade the reader to the author's point of view. The images of prosperous farmsteads in county atlases usually appear because the farmers who owned them paid to have them published. Trade catalogs list wholesale prices, leaving customer prices to each retailer's discretion. Community brochures promoted boosterism. Everything comes with bias, so be cautious and skeptical at all times.

## Unpublished Primary Documents

These are unique documents that were created for a specific purpose, like record keeping. A major category of unpublished primary documents is public records, which are documents or pieces of information that are not considered confidential and generally pertain to the conduct of government. This is a large and crucial category of documentation for local history research. Much of this information is filed in public records offices, often county courthouses. Many of these documents are now accessible online on searchable databases, often on websites that have been created for researching family genealogy. Particularly useful public records for researching time, place, and people for historical environments include:

- US Census records, collected at the end of each decade. Population census records began in 1790 and are available for public viewing up to 1940 (except those from 1890, most of which were unfortunately destroyed by fire in 1921). Some states also collected census information. Agriculture and manufacturing census records were also collected through various decades of the nineteenth century. Census records are incredibly valuable to research time, place, and people. But they can be hard to read because they were often handwritten, and they can contain inaccurate spellings of names. They also often missed people, especially members of minority groups. Primarily because they are difficult to read, census records that have been transcribed for online databases often contain errors as well.

- Land and property records, proving ownership and transfers of property.
- Tax records showing increases in land values, which often denoted the building of a structure on a property.
- Wills and probate records, which can include inventories of personal belongings at the time of one's death.
- Vital records, including births, marriages, divorces, and deaths.
- Court records of lawsuits, criminal activity, and other transactions.
- Military records.
- Records of the US Patent and Trademark Office, since 1790 (available online).
- Records of the US Post Office Department, with listings of postmaster appointments and names and locations of post offices (on microfilm at the National Archives, searchable via an online index).
- Records of the US Customs Bureau (on microfilm at the National Archives, searchable via an online index).

Other useful unpublished primary documents for researching historical environments include:

- Personal and family papers, letters, journals, diaries, and scrapbooks.
- County and municipal government records.
- Community organization records, including those from churches, labor unions, political parties, service clubs, philanthropic and fraternal organizations, and the Social Register.
- Business records, including accounts, inventories, meeting minutes, and correspondence.
- Records of Dun and Bradstreet (originally R. G. Dun), providing detailed information on American businesses in order to rate the suitability of these businesses for credit, 1841–1892 (online finding aid at the Baker Library, Harvard Business School).
- Cemetery records, some of which appear on https://www.findagrave.com/.

If not otherwise noted above, these sources are increasingly available through online databases or identified through finding aids in local archives, libraries, universities, and historical societies. Like published primary sources, always check with the repositories in the local area you are researching to possibly reveal a source that is not on the Internet.

Unpublished primary documents are advantageous in that they often include data on demographics, social stratification, occupations, and household composition. But, for this same reason, they also have disadvantages. They are all simply bits of data that need to be compared and contrasted, assessed and analyzed, and compared with other sources. Furthermore, they provide little insight into attitudes, mindset, and potential ways in which individuals within groups responded to social, economic, and political changes. These sources can contain factual inaccuracies as well.

## Visual Documents[12]

These types of primary documents can be incredibly valuable tools for researching time, place, and people for your historical environment. They comprise:

- Maps—a rich source of information, including plat maps showing the exact dimensions and layout of a piece of land (often part of a deed or land record); Sanborn Fire Insurance Maps, depicting layout, shape, and use of structures in cities and towns, published beginning in 1867 (online access through Library of Congress); county atlas maps; hand-drawn property maps; and bird's-eye-view lithographs of towns and villages, popular between the 1870s and 1920s. The detail of some of these is quite extensive, while others will likely leave you disappointed because of their sketchiness and inaccuracies.
- Sketches, paintings, and other artwork (particularly useful during the era before photography).
- Architectural drawings and plans.
- Photographs, beginning earlier but particularly from the 1860s on (see Figure 4.2).

Visual documents like paintings and photographs are excellent sources for showing how people dressed, the settings within which they lived and worked, how they conveyed proper etiquette and deportment of their time, and the accoutrements of their daily lives. Visual sources make extremely valuable complements to written sources. But keep in mind that they are mediated documents. People usually consciously dressed and posed for them. Artists and photographers brought their own biases to the subjects and the ways in which they portrayed their subjects. Caution must be used to assess what they are, why they were created, and who created them. Always question how accurate,

Figure 4.2. Studying historic photographs like this one, circa 1895, helped with numerous details in the arrangement and furnishing of the J. R. Jones Store.
Courtesy of The Henry Ford

manipulated, and documented the visual source is. Also, beware of historical advertisements and other visual documents on sites like Google Images and Flickr, as many do not mention date or provenance. These sites are, however, occasionally useful for offering leads through keyword searches that can take you to better documented information.

## Oral Histories[13]

These types of primary documents involve "the systematic collection and recording of personal memories as historical documentation."[14] They have the advantage of supplementing written records by filling in gaps. Oral histories usually involve recording a live, in-person interview in audio or video format, then transcribing and summarizing the interview. They can also take the form of written reminiscences, such as slave narratives, Great Depression oral history projects, and regional local history initiatives. Some of these have been transcribed and are available online or through online databases and finding aids.

The advantages of oral histories are many. They can be highly engaging to the public because they express how people feel about something and convey a level of detail not available in other sources. As eyewitness accounts of events that took place in the past, oral histories can be informative, vivid, and colorful. They can enliven a larger narrative, add a touch of humor, show common or contested threads among groups, and provide a welcome change of pace to the often dry data of statistics and demographic information. They are, of course, particularly valuable for recent history, where synthesized versions of the history do not yet exist but people are still around to recount an era and supply missing information if records are incomplete.

But oral histories are highly subjective as well. They can conflict with written sources, presenting a problem to the researcher. It is not unusual for people being interviewed about the same event to disagree with each other over the details, as personal memories of the past can be greatly divergent. Oral history interviews are fraught with bias, as interviewees might purposely leave out part of the story, focus on trivial details, show disregard for following a standard chronology, compress or telescope time, or change the story for their own purposes. In addition, personal memories are imprecise and can even change over time. Interviewers can also add their own biases, asking leading and loaded questions and bringing certain attitudes, beliefs, preconceived notions, and personal interests of their own. It is best to combine the use of oral history sources with other sources.

Also keep in mind that recording, transcribing, and summarizing oral histories take a great deal of time and resources. One must consider the value of undertaking a project like this before getting started. It is best to check for any previously implemented oral histories related to your project, in published form or online. Before starting an oral history project, it is crucial to know exactly what you are trying to find out. In the course of interviewing someone, it is easy for the conversation to veer off track. It takes as much rigor to get what you want out of an oral interview than out of other research sources—just a different kind of rigor. Useful books exist on planning and implementing oral histories.[15]

## Material Culture Evidence[16]

With scant or no written records at hand, archaeologists were the first specialists to develop methodologies for uncovering the rich social and cultural meanings behind manmade artifacts. Material culture—defined as "the tangible things crafted, shaped, altered, and used across time and space by humans"— can reveal insights into socioeconomic conditions, political circumstances, and cultural norms with an immediacy that documents do not.[17] Within the context of a historical environment, artifacts—with their underlying meanings— provide a powerful window into past lives and cultural mindset.

As a research source, artifacts should be approached similarly to other sources—with a series of questions. What is it? Who made it? Why was it made? How does it relate to other artifacts of its time and place? What does it reveal about individual and cultural mindset? How does it complement other research sources to reveal these things?[18] Consider inherent biases. Are you certain that it is an authentic artifact from that era? Does it truly reflect the time, place, and people you wish to represent (as opposed to coming from outside of the region, from a different era, or from a higher socioeconomic level than you are intending)? Artifacts are one of the most concrete and visceral components of a historical environment, highly engaging and powerful to visitors. You will want to make sure that you have a solid research foundation to back up the decisions you make as you consider the place of material culture in your furnishings plan (see chapter 5).

### The Physical Structure as a Primary Document[19]

Finally, if you are creating an environment within a historic structure, a careful examination of the structure itself—interior, exterior, and change over time—can provide vast amounts of information. Materials, design, and construction techniques can reveal much about the attitudes and mindset, traditions and values of people living in a time and place. It is helpful to get input on this from experts in "reading" historic structures, who can pinpoint and interpret minute structural changes and help reconstruct the building's history. Buildings also can be particularly hard to decipher—even misleading—without documentary evidence to back up their physical changes through time (see Figure 4.3).

### The Research Report

This written report summarizes all your research findings, with bibliographic citations. Some historic sites include a historic structure report as part of this, or incorporate their research into a furnishings plan (which I will describe at length in chapter 5).[20] However you decide to do it, don't put it off! It's best to write up your research findings—the data you've uncovered, the conclusions you've drawn from that data, and the sources you used—while they are still fresh in your mind.

The following real-life examples illustrate how the preceding research methodologies can apply to historical environments from three different time periods, places, and cultural contexts. While similar types of sources were used, the research questions and eras of interpretation drove the ways in which each research methodology was pursued.

**Figure 4.3.** An analysis of the general store structure revealed such information as the original placement of windows, doors, stairwells, and shelving, as well as additions and changes over time. This photograph is of the store about to move from its original location in Waterford, Michigan, to Greenfield Village in 1927.
Courtesy of The Henry Ford

## RESEARCH METHODOLOGY FOR McGUFFEY BIRTHPLACE (INTERPRETED 1800–1802)[21]

The log home birthplace of William Holmes McGuffey (the creator of *McGuffey Readers*), built 1798, dates from a time and place for which few published primary sources or visual documents exist. Delving into unpublished primary sources provided the best clues to addressing the research questions. Fortunately, we received unexpected assistance on this.

This historic structure was originally located in West Finley Township near Claysville, Washington County, Pennsylvania. When what remained of it was moved to and reconstructed in Greenfield Village during the 1930s, the home was furnished as a "typical" pioneer log cabin with the addition of a few items from later McGuffey family descendants. To coincide with a proposed restoration of the structure, historical research was initiated to determine a more accurate and focused interpretation of the building. The period of 1800–1802 was chosen as the date of interpretation, to represent the small window of time after which William Holmes McGuffey was born, but before the McGuffey family packed up their belongings and moved farther west to the Ohio frontier.

## Research Questions

These questions framed the research methodology:

1. How might families of Scots-Irish heritage have lived their daily lives in the then-frontier area of southwestern Pennsylvania around 1800?
2. How might families of Scots-Irish heritage have furnished a log home in this time and place? What traditions might they have brought from their homeland? What adaptations might the family have made within their new environment?
3. How much can we know about the McGuffey family specifically, especially their time living here? Were they typical or atypical of other families like themselves?
4. Were there aspects of William Holmes McGuffey's heritage and upbringing that might have influenced his later creation of his *Readers*, and how might these be suggested in the home?

The following sources proved to be most helpful:

### Step 1: Secondary Sources

A few biographies of William Holmes McGuffey were written, though quite long ago and primarily for the purpose of commemoration. Fortunately, scholarly works on Scots-Irish immigration to America—particularly the book *The Scotch-Irish: A Social History*—offered better, more accurate historical information, as did books and articles on the history of log houses and immigration to the Appalachian frontier.[22]

### Step 2: Census Records

It was easy enough to check the 1800 population census to offer a bit of information about the McGuffey family, but more in-depth primary source research about the lifestyles and furnishings habits of Scots-Irish families in southwestern Pennsylvania needed to be done.

*Step 3: Research Study of Scots-Irish Families*
*in Washington County, Pennsylvania*

Serendipitously, we learned that another project similar to ours was being undertaken at the same time: the research and reinstallation of the Miller House at Meadowcroft Museum of Rural Life (now Meadowcroft Rockshelter and Historic Village) in Avella, Washington County, Pennsylvania. We learned that Meadowcroft's consulting historian, Jennifer Ford, had developed a set of research questions that centered around exploring exactly what we were looking for—the unique characteristics of Scots-Irish homes and their furnishings, particularly as they varied from their Pennsylvania German neighbors.[23] We were extremely fortunate that Jennifer offered to check the sources she was using to see what she could uncover about the background, habitation, and furnishings of the McGuffey family.

As a professionally trained historian, Jennifer's research methodology was well crafted and substantive. For her cross-section study of Scots-Irish families, her research sources included:

- Several hundred probate inventories (in the Washington and Westmoreland County courthouses) as well as auction lists of property (on microfilm) of families with Scots-Irish surnames. She cross-referenced these with store ledgers, newspaper advertisements, contemporary descriptions, and extant artifacts.
- Township tax records to reconstruct the built landscape of the area. This included a taxable list for men in the county in 1800. An important source was a special Federal Direct Tax Census undertaken in 1798, a one-time-only assessment mandated by Congress of every privately owned property in every township across the young nation.
- Scholarly works on traditional arrangements of farmsteads, buildings, and interior spaces in the northern Irish province of Ulster, and in Appalachia, to see what Scots-Irish customs survived longest in America.

For the McGuffey family specifically, her research sources included:

- The 1798 Federal Direct Tax Census for land value, dwelling value, and a comparison with other families, which uncovered a great deal of information about both the McGuffey and Holmes families (William Holmes McGuffey's mother's family and also the owners of the property on which this log home was situated).

- The 1800 taxable list for men in the county.
- Unfortunately, no probate inventory for the McGuffey family existed, although Jennifer had already developed a "basic household tool kit" from twenty-five Scots-Irish families living in Washington and Westmoreland Counties between 1798 and 1803, which she provided to us.

## Summary of Findings

*Research Question 1: How might families of Scots-Irish heritage have lived their daily lives in the frontier area of Southwestern Pennsylvania around 1800?*

As a result of her research, the word Jennifer used to describe the Scots-Irish population in the area was "adaptive." Lacking the language barrier of German families, they acculturated more easily. In specific categories related to farming, the German families in her study did outweigh the Scots-Irish: they had larger barns and outbuildings, more tools, more crops and orchards, and more acres of land clustered together in one place. But the Scots-Irish farmers were not poor or indifferent. They were, for the most part, good farmers, using the tools that were at their disposal.

From this study, Jennifer also concluded that, despite the characteristic of adaptiveness, Scots-Irish families did not leave all of their Old World ideas and ways of doing things behind. They shared a similar heritage of such traditions as music, language, foodways, and material culture. They also tried to establish familiar institutions in the move west—first churches, but also schools, stores, and courts of law. However, the constant movement of people into new territory threatened the maintenance of cultural traditions and family heritage, and marked a shift toward the importance of individual achievement as an indicator of status in the community.

*Research Question 2: How might families of Scots-Irish heritage have furnished a log home in this time and place? What traditions might they have brought from their homeland? What might constitute adaptations to their new environment?*

From her study of inventories, Jennifer found that there were definite retentions of tradition in interior spaces by these families. Most important was their continuing use of interior space like their Ulster ancestors—with a pathway kept clear between the entrance and the hearth, which was the focal point and social center of the home. Other traditions included the husband and wife each occupying a specific side of the room, the bed serving as a prominent feature in the room, and the dresser (or cupboard) maintaining a ubiquitous presence in the room as a place to store and proudly display household possessions.

*Research Question 3: How much can we know about the McGuffey family specifically, especially their time living here? Were they typical or atypical of other families like them?*

Interestingly, William Holmes McGuffey's parents seem to have fit the two extremes of the spectrum for the Scots-Irish profile. William's mother, Anna, was like others who preferred to stay in the more settled communities, valuing stability, family bonds, viable institutions, community control of morality, the amenities of social interaction, decency and order, and the worth of tradition. Anna McGuffey was the influence behind William's formal schooling and lifelong love of learning. In contrast, his restless father Alexander was among those who preferred the values of individualism, adventure, independence of action, taking risks, and making one's own way in the world.

*Research Question 4: Were there aspects of William Holmes McGuffey's heritage and upbringing that might have influenced the later creation of his* Readers, *and how might these be portrayed in the home?*

Comparing the primary sources from Jennifer Ford with the biographies of William Holmes McGuffey, it was now possible to begin to address this question. William was nurtured on the emerging frontier but better educated than most—two experiences that influenced his entire life and career.

These findings would all play a role in the interpretive strategy and furnishings plan to come (see chapters 5 and 6).

## RESEARCH METHODOLOGY FOR J. R. JONES GENERAL STORE (INTERPRETED 1882–1888)[24]

This example took advantage of the prolific variety of sources for this topic and era, including published and unpublished primary documents, visual documents, material culture evidence, and the structure itself. Selected secondary sources were also helpful while an unpublished reminiscence of J. R. Jones himself added key information.

### Research Questions

Planning for the J. R. Jones General Store occurred over a period of some three years, as delays in the installation due to lack of funding actually aided in the ability to do substantive research. Throughout the course of the planning for this project, specific research questions continually evolved and often were being addressed simultaneously. These were the five research questions that evolved over the course of the project:

1. What time, place, and storekeeper is best for us to interpret (that is, with the best documentation, the best alignment with our existing collections, the best interpretive potential, and the closest alignment with mission)?
2. What was the role of the J. R. Jones Store in the local community?
3. How were stores like this laid out?
4. What products were stocked on the shelves?
5. What kind of value and meaning did individual products, or groups of products, have to people living in the community during this era?

*Question 1: Time, Place, and Storekeeper*

We decided early on that, although the store sign came from upstate New York, the store itself was a real building from a real place—the rural cross-roads village of Waterford, Oakland County, Michigan. For this reason we decided to focus on the role of this general store in the Waterford, Michigan, community. The following primary sources proved to be most helpful:

- Tax records—revealed an increased value of the property in 1857–1858, likely reflecting the construction of the store at that time.
- US Post Office Department records—gave us a list of postmasters in Waterford, a task that storekeepers generally assumed in a community based upon their political affiliation with the current US president. Some of the postmasters in Waterford over time matched the names of storekeepers of this store gleaned from other sources.
- Dun and Bradstreet records—told us about credit ratings of several of the storekeepers who ran this store and confirmed their names and dates.
- Annual editions of the *Michigan State Gazetteer and Business Directory*—included year-by-year listings of Waterford residents and their occupations.
- *Pontiac Bill Poster* newspaper—Waterford did not have its own newspaper, but this newspaper was published in the larger, nearby town of Pontiac. Reporters in small communities located near Pontiac contributed weekly columns to this newspaper, including Waterford. These columns revealed much information about local residents and events, and occasionally provided insight into our own store and storekeepers.
- Population census records—confirmed the names of storekeepers in town every ten years (except 1890 because of the loss of records to fire).

From these sources, we constructed a probable history of the storekeepers at our store and the likely years they ran the business. We found that the store-keepers of our store changed hands often (nine times to be exact between the

1850s and 1927), and later learned that this likely occurred because store-keeping did not involve much up-front capital and it was a risky business. Many storekeepers tended to try it for a while, then move on.

Selecting James R. Jones as "our" storekeeper (time period, from 1882 to 1888) resulted from the combination of most consistent documentation between sources, more extensive documentation than the other storekeepers, and a beneficial era for us to interpret (as described in chapter 3). We had also found in our files a transcript of J. R. Jones's visit to Greenfield Village after the building was moved there in 1927, with his personal reminiscences of the store, its products, and his storekeeping business. Further primary research on J. R. Jones included his probate, which postdated this era so unfortunately did not contain useful information for us, and an extremely helpful obituary for him from the Holly, Michigan, newspaper. This obituary confirmed much information we already knew and revealed a few more tidbits.

## *Question 2: The Role of This Store in Waterford, Michigan*

After the initial Project Brief was approved (see chapter 3), we decided that it was important for us to know what strategies Jones would have adopted to attract customers to the store—for example, what kinds of products Jones might have stocked there, what other functions the store would have served, and who the potential customers were and what their lives were like (relating to the front-end evaluation). This question also would help us get at a deeper interpretation of products on the shelves than a simple display. For this we created a community profile using the following primary sources:

- Population census records—listed people who lived in the village of Waterford and their occupations as well as residents of the surrounding agricultural community.
- Agricultural census records—to discern what farmers in this agricultural community grew and raised, to know what products were available in the local community and what farm families might have brought into the store for credit.
- Michigan State Gazetteers—for annual listings of local residents and their occupations.
- County atlases of 1872, 1896, and 1908—listed Waterford businesses; showed plat maps of the village, township and county; and depicted the farmsteads of the more prosperous farmers.
- Oakland County histories published in 1877, 1912, and 1925—described prominent citizens and other aspects of Waterford history.

- Weekly Waterford columns in the *Pontiac Bill Poster* newspaper—an invaluable document of local residents' comings and goings, the personalities of select individuals, and—because of its chatty nature—insight into the community's values and mindset.

From these sources, we concluded that Waterford, though rural, was not an isolated community but was closely interconnected with outlying villages and towns, as well as the city of Detroit, thirty-five miles away. During most of its history, Waterford supported several stores, some more specialized than others. Later, using this rich body of material, we created actual profiles of several potential customers to the store, to help us think creatively about what kinds of products community members might have been interested in purchasing.

We next decided that we needed broader-context information about people's mindset and attitudes within a community like Waterford, so we delved into scholarly secondary literature to address such topics as:

- Farmer's issues of the time;
- City/country connections;
- Middle-class values;
- The nature of social class in a village like Waterford;
- Characteristics of an established rural community;
- The nature of politics in Waterford at this time.

Each of these "issues" was synthesized into a written report, with bibliographic sources, for future reference.

*Question 3: Store Layout*

To address this question, we collected as many visual documents of historic store interiors from around the era of our research as possible. Some were published in secondary sources (published photographic essays of towns and villages were particularly helpful) and in museum archives. It was crucial to get an exact date and provenance on these, in order to know what images dated from later than our era (for example, showing a great increase in canned goods) and what images were for more specialized—not "general merchandise"—stores (for example, dry goods, groceries, and hardware). These images could all be useful, but their distinctions needed to be taken into account. We studied the details of each of these to discern patterns (for example, a showcase with boxes of cigars appeared in the front left corner of several store images). The major pattern we found was that product arrangements in general merchandise stores were not random and chaotic but organized and orderly, divided into distinctive so-called "departments" (see Figure 4.2).

### Question 4: Store Products

Lacking a specific inventory and images of the J. R. Jones Store from the 1880s, we researched what we considered the next best thing—store accounts from similar stores in close proximity and time period to our store from an extensive collection of these in the Bentley Historical Library, University of Michigan, Ann Arbor. For this project, we chose four general stores in southern Michigan that aligned with our store in terms of time period, types of products, geographical proximity, and village profile. A study and database analysis of the daybooks and inventories revealed such rich information as names of products and their units of measure, quantities sold, retail prices, items brought in for credit, increase over time of brand name products versus bulk products, system of payment, and monthly and seasonal variations (see Figure 4.4). Comparing these with the visual images, we began to divide our findings into several discreet categories of goods or "departments," including groceries, tobacco, boots and shoes, hardware, agricultural equipment, housewares, clothing and accessories, and dry goods. This would help us later in developing the store layout and furnishings plan.

Other sources we used to research potential store products included:

- Product advertisements from the *Pontiac Bill Poster* newspaper (see Figure 4.1).
- The *Grocer's Companion and Merchant's Handbook* of 1883—an invaluable compendium of information about store products.
- Material culture evidence—through a cataloging project documenting our own extensive general store collections that had been acquired during Henry Ford's era (about 5,000 objects), with makers, places of manufacture, and dates.
- Trade catalogs of the era offered a wealth of visual information about the objects in the general store accounts, newspaper advertisements, *Grocer's Companion*, and objects in our collection. These also included wholesale prices for each object and showed myriad varieties of types of objects that helped with dating existing objects in our collection and helping us determine additional objects to acquire.
- Internet research—over time, has allowed us to delve more deeply into the histories of individual objects, through patent records, company and town histories, and digitized object records and blog posts about similar objects in other museum collections.

Figure 4.4. When the study of general store daybooks showed that stores like the J. R. Jones Store stocked numerous specialized fabrics—especially for women's clothing and domestic textiles—several bolts of reproduction fabrics representing this vast assortment were created and stocked on the shelves. The display of gloves, also based upon daybook accounts, are historic artifacts.

Photo by Deborah Berk

*Question 5: Value and Meaning of Products to Store Customers*

This question was intended to get at the deeper social and cultural meanings of the products so that our interpretation (and potential choices of objects on the shelves) would move beyond simply placing objects on display to truly viewing each of them as concrete windows into people's daily lives. To accomplish this, we came up with about thirty topics—ranging from Lydia Pinkham's medicine to laundry bluing to ladies' collars—then we delved deeply into primary sources like advice and etiquette books, how-to books, and house furnishings books to begin to unearth the deeper meaning of these from an era during which people's attitudes and mindset differed from our own. A synthesis of each topic was written into a summarized "material culture" report, including bibliographic sources.

## Summary of Findings

With the findings of our five research questions in hand, we felt that we had an adequate foundation of research on storekeeper J. R. Jones, his customers, and the types and arrangement of products he stocked in his store. Our next move was to develop an interpretive strategy and furnishings plan (see chapter 5).

## RESEARCH METHODOLOGY FOR "BACK-TO-THE-LAND" COMMUNE, *YOUR PLACE IN TIME* EXHIBITION (INTERPRETED 1973)

This example was unusual in that it dated from a fairly recent era. While it seems that this would be advantageous, the research turned out to be fairly challenging. In the end, the best findings focused upon a specific type of published source, one invaluable visual source, and a selection of oral histories and written reminiscences.

## Research Questions

Since this was to be a representative environment—not an actual structure moved to the exhibition—the research methodology focused upon overall impressions and patterns related to these types of environments in the late 1960s and early 1970s. The research questions were:

1. What were the attitudes and mindset of people who lived in these places? Would this help us determine a more specific date for the environment?

2. How were these spaces furnished and how were people's attitudes and mindset reflected in the furnishings of these spaces?

*Step 1: Published Books and Articles by Outside Observers*

Because this was such a recent era of history, we started with the *Readers' Guide to Periodical Literature*, a reference guide to popular general-interest periodicals. We found a long listing of magazine articles contemporary to the era listed under the heading, "Collective Settlements." These articles appeared in such magazines as *Life*, *Look*, *Ebony*, *McCall's*, *New York Times Magazine*, *Saturday Review*, and *Time*. A few books from that era that described commune life, written by journalists, were also referenced.

We then tracked down copies of several of these articles and books. As we were perusing them, however, we felt that there seemed to be something amiss with them. Authors of these articles tended to treat the topic—and the people living in these places—with a rather derisive tone. We realized the problem was that these authors (and their intended readers) were what we came to think of as "outsiders" to the culture and mindset of communal, "back-to-the-land" living. While these articles were intriguing, they were only going to help us so far with our research questions.

*Step 2: Published Materials by "Insiders"*

Therefore we looked for sources that came directly from "insiders," starting with the *Whole Earth Catalog* and literature referenced in that publication, then branching out to such sources as *Mother Earth News*, *Lifestyle* magazine, and books about building alternative living structures. We also looked at accounts of communal living from the era written by "insiders."

*Step 3: Visual Documents*

Finding visual images of communal living spaces from this era was crucial to connecting this planned exhibition component with our larger exhibition goals and the attitudes and mindset we read about in the "insider" sources of the era. We found a few photographs in published compendiums of the era but these seemed to be purposefully posed, intended to serve as photojournalistic pieces and, as such, might have been staged, contrived, or otherwise mediated.

Fortunately, we found the 1973 book *Shelter*, which offered page after page of seemingly more spontaneously photographed communal spaces and people living in these spaces.[25] We pored over these photographs, analyzing the layouts and individual objects in them, trying to discern patterns, trends, and key iconic objects in the scenes (see Figure 4.5).

Figure 4.5. Numerous images of living spaces in the *Shelter* publication conveyed evidence of back-to-the-landers' embrace of earlier technologies, such as this coal-burning stove installed in the 1973 commune environment in the *Your Place in Time* exhibition, Henry Ford Museum of American Innovation.

Photo by Deborah Berk

*Step 4: Oral Histories and Written Reminiscences*

We determined that we did not have time or resources to undertake a major oral history project related to this. But we did interview several individuals who had lived in these spaces about both the backgrounds and motivations of people who chose this type of living as well as specific furnishings questions. For example, a question posed to a group of interviewees via email about the record albums that people living in these places might have owned led to a spirited debate between informants.

## A Word about Internet Resources

In some ways, the Internet may be easier for researching earlier history than this more recent era, as many institutions are digitizing older collections, local history sources, and archival documents rather than more recent materials. However, it is possible to find your way to many recent sources if you know how to look for them. The *Readers' Guide to Periodical Literature*, an important index of recent popular periodicals, is now available as an online database. Popular magazines of the 1970s have often been microfilmed and are listed in online catalogs of public libraries. Some magazines have been digitized. Others might be obtained from online used book dealers. Names of books and published accounts of communal life from the era can often be found by searching key words, leading to books that have been reprinted, digitized, sold by used book dealers, or accessible from public libraries through interlibrary loan. Academic articles are searchable and accessible through online databases. Topics like the history of geodesic domes appear on many websites, often with bibliographic sources. Visual images are tricky because they are often undated but can provide leads to better documented materials. YouTube videos of historic commercials and mass media programming from the era can be helpful. The key is to always make sure the sources are documented, date specifically to the era, and adequately address your research questions.

## Summary of Findings

*Research Question 1: What were the attitudes and mindset of people who lived in these places? Would this help us determine a more specific date for the environment?*

The key to this question was finding the "insider" perspectives, comparing them, and looking for patterns. After perusing the various sources described above, the date of 1973 was determined for this environment because it represented a peak of the back-to-the-land movement of this era, when multiple and varied strategies for communal living were attempted. It was an era during which the back-to-the-land movement went "mainstream" if you will, before people who lived in these places got burned out or disillusioned.

*Research Question 2: How were these spaces furnished and how were people's attitudes and mindset reflected in the furnishings of these spaces?*
The written, visual, and oral history sources revealed several patterns which would help us create the environment, showing, for example, that:

- Most (though not all) of the people who lived in these places were young, educated, and typically from a higher socioeconomic class than the mainstream.
- The people who lived in these places overtly expressed a rejection of their parents' and general middle-class Americans' lifestyles by adopting such practices as: using castoff furnishings, making handcrafted items, embracing earlier forms of technology, and choosing alternative foods and ingredients.
- The people who lived here shared a similar outlook to each other in terms of pursuing this experimental way of living as well as in adopting certain lifestyle choices.

As the result of perusals through numerous sources from the era, we knew that we would be creating one representative approach to living communally in the exhibition space. Some of our furnishings choices would specifically reference visual images and other sources we found, while other choices would reflect general trends and patterns that aligned with our goals. Since we had no artifacts for this space to begin with, we felt that we had the opportunity to consider that each item we acquired and planned for this space could embody one or more of the above characteristics and reveal insight into both personal values and cultural mindset.

## HISTORICAL RESEARCH: A CRUCIAL STEP

Your research methodology is a challenging, though crucial, step in creating your historical environment. The rigorous attention to detail you pay in your historical research provides a firm backbone of believability and authenticity to the final environment you create. As demonstrated in the three real-life examples in this chapter, a range of sources—secondary, primary, visual, oral, material culture, and the physical structure—can aid in the creation of your research methodology. Each type of source comes with pros and cons of which you should be aware and take into account. Chances are that you will go back and forth throughout your research process between different types of sources. This is fine and expected, in fact desirable. Each project comes with different parameters and needs, as seen in the three examples. But, except for some variation across time, the major types of sources remain fairly constant. At all times, it is best to have a research plan before you begin, know what your questions are, be aware of what each source can and cannot tell you, and be open to changing course if need be.

## NOTES

1. Cherstin M. Lyon, Elizabeth M. Nix, and Rebecca K. Shrum, *Introduction to Public History: Interpreting the Past, Engaging Audiences* (Lanham, MD: Rowman & Littlefield, 2007), 2.

2. Ibid.

3. In "Part II: Research design and methodology for a new interpretation of the Miller House," of a three-part article written by Daniel J. Freas, Jennifer L. Ford, and David. R. Scofield, *Proceedings of the 1997 Conference and Annual Meeting, Staunton, Virginia*, ed. Debra A. Reid, vol. XX (North Bloomfield, OH: The Association for Living Historical Farms and Agricultural Museums, 1998): 201.

4. David E. Kyvig and Myron A. Marty, *Nearby History: Exploring the Past Around You*, 3rd ed. (Lanham, MD: AltaMira Press, a Division of Rowman & Littlefield, 2010), 20–43. Detailed lists of questions are organized into the following categories: The Family, Places of Residence, Neighborhoods, Organizations, Community, and Functional Categories.

5. Lyon, Nix, and Shrum, *Introduction to Public History*, 23–24.

6. Ibid., 26. Another example of this can be found in "Living History Farm Research Tips, Table 1: Type of Source and Information Contained," accessed December 11, 2017, http://www.alhfam.org/living-history-farms-resources#LHF2.

7. Lyon, Nix, and Shrum, *Introduction to Public History*, 26–27.

8. For Internet research advantages and cautions, see Kyvig and Marty, *Nearby History*, 51.

9. For more questions intended to unearth bias related to secondary sources, see Phyllis K. Leffler and Joseph Brent, *Public History Readings, Application II: Secondary Sources* (Malabar, FL: Krieger Publishing Co., 1992), 212.

10. More in-depth explanations, as well as pros and cons, of a range of primary sources can be found in Kyvig and Marty, *Nearby History*, 61–111; and Barbara J. Howe, Dolores A. Fleming, Emory L. Kemp, and Ruth Ann Overbeck, *Houses and Homes: Exploring Their History*, The Nearby History Series, vol. 2 (Nashville, TN: American Association for State and Local History, 1987), 39–58. Although intended for genealogical research, the site www.familysearch.org (especially the link https://www.familysearch.org/wiki/en/United_States_Genealogy) contains easy-to-understand descriptions of many different primary sources. See also "General Guide

to Sources," a National Register Bulletin on Researching a Historic Property, US Department of the Interior, National Park Service, accessed August 15, 2018, https://www.nps.gov/nr/publications/bulletins/nrb39/nrb39_IV.htm.

11. "What Are Primary Sources?" UC Irvine Libraries, accessed August 12, 2018, https://www.lib.uci.edu/what-are-primary-sources.

12. For more background, see Kyvig and Marty, *Nearby History*, 133–57; and Howe, Fleming, Kemp, and Overbeck, *Houses and Homes*, 65–72.

13. The many excellent sources describing oral histories and their methodology include Donald A. Ritchie, *Doing Oral History: A Practical Guide*, 3rd ed. (New York: Oxford University Press, 2015); and Barbara Allen Bogart, "Using Oral History in Museums," *History News* 50, no. 4 (Autumn 1995): Technical Leaflet #191. See also Kyvig and Marty, *Nearby History*, 113–32.

14. Bogart, *Using Oral History*, 2.

15. See sources listed in footnote 13. Donald Ritchie's *Doing Oral History: A Practical Guide* is particularly in-depth.

16. Sources describing the use of material culture as a source include *Material Culture Studies in America*, ed. Thomas J. Schlereth (Lanham, MD: AltaMira Press, a Division of Rowman & Littlefield, 1999); Jules David Prown, "Mind in Matter: An Introduction to Material Culture Theory and Method," *Winterthur Portfolio* 17, no. 1 (Spring 1982): 1–19; Mary Johnson, "What's in a Butterchurn or a Sadiron? Some Thoughts on Using Artifacts in Social History," *The Public Historian* 5, no. 1 (Winter 1983): 60–81; and Simon J. Bronner, "The Idea of the Folk Artifact," in *Public History Readings*, 222–23. For pros and cons of using this source for research, see Kyvig and Marty, *Nearby History*, 159–75.

17. Bronner, "The Idea of the Folk Artifact," 222.

18. Excellent methodologies for analyzing and discerning meaning behind material culture artifacts are described in E. McClung Fleming, "Artifact Study: A Proposed Model," *Winterthur Portfolio* 9, no. 4 (1974): 153–73; and Kenneth L. Ames, "Meaning in Artifacts: Hall Furnishings in Victorian America," *Journal of Interdisciplinary History* 9 (Summer 1978): 19–46.

19. Strategies for analyzing historic structures as a research source are addressed in Howe, Fleming, Kemp, and Overbeck, *Houses and Homes*, 23–38.

20. Examples in which research findings are incorporated into furnishings plans include William Seale, *Recreating the Historic House Interior* (Nashville, TN: American Association for State and Local History, 1979); Martha B. Katz-Hyman and Mick Woodcock, "The Basics of Writing Furnishings Plans," *Proceedings of the 2000 Conference and Annual Meeting, Mystic, Connecticut*, ed. Ron Kley and Jane Radcliffe, vol. XXIII (North Bloomfield, OH: The Association for Living History, Farm and Agricultural Museums, 2001): 158–62; Bradley Brooks, "The Historic House Furnishings Plan: Process and Product," *Interpreting Historic House Museums*, ed. Jessica Foy Donnelly (Lanham, MD: AltaMira Press, a Division of Rowman & Littlefield, 2002): 128–43; and "Guidelines for Preparing Historic Furnishings Reports," National Park Service Harpers Ferry Center, accessed March 21, 2018, https://www.nps.gov/hfc/products/furnish/furnish-plan-hfr-guide.cfm.

21. This case study drew from the following unpublished manuscripts: "Preliminary Historic Structure Report, William Holmes McGuffey Birthplace" (13 September 1989); "The McGuffey Birthplace: Updated Information for a Proposed New Program" (5 June 15); "McGuffey Birthplace Program Proposal" (July 1998); "McGuffey Web Component" (2003); and "William Holmes McGuffey Historic Presenter Training Manual" (2003), Donna Braden Papers, Benson Ford Research Center, The Henry Ford, Dearborn, MI (hereafter cited as Braden Papers).

22. James G. Leyburn, *The Scotch-Irish: A Social History* (Chapel Hill: University of North Carolina Press, 1962).

23. Jennifer Ford's methodology and research findings were published in the article by Daniel J. Freas, Jennifer L. Ford, and David. R. Scofield, "Chinking Between the Logs: Reinterpreting the Miller House at Meadowcroft Museum of Rural Life," *Proceedings of the 1997 Conference and Annual Meeting, Staunton, Virginia*, ed. Debra A. Reid, vol. XX (North Bloomfield, OH: The Association for Living Historical Farms and Agricultural Museums, 1998): 200–205.

24. This case study was drawn from the following published article: Donna R. Braden, "The Process and the Product: Transforming the General Store in Greenfield Village," *History News* 50, no. 3 (Summer 1995): 20–24; and the following unpublished manuscripts: "General Store Project, Historic Structure Report, Report #1" (7 November 1990); "General Store Project Plan" (9 September 1991); "General Store Reinstallation Project, Review of Assumptions" (23 January 1992); "General Store Project: Proposal Restatement/Program Brief" (1 May 1992, rev. 29 May, 1992); "History of the General Store Building/Getting the History Right" (n.d., ca. 1993); "The J. R. Jones General Store in Greenfield Village, Program Plan" (15 September 1992); "J. R. Jones General Store Presenter Training Manual" (April 1994); and handout to presenters at J. R. Jones General Store training refresh (6 April 2016), Braden Papers.

25. *Shelter* (Bolinas, CA: Shelter Publications), written by Lloyd Kahn and Bob Easton, was first published in 1973. Kahn had previously worked as an editor for the *Whole Earth Catalog*. Over the next three years, *Shelter* proved so popular that it was reprinted twice and sold 185,000 copies. An identical edition to the original classic book was reprinted in 1990 (distributed by New York: Random House) and a second edition was printed in 2000. According to the 1990 edition, its purpose was "to show a wide range of information on hand-built housing and the building crafts and to maintain a network of people interested in building and shelter, with subsequent publication of the best available information." The book is still in print and has a related website, Shelter Online, at https://www.shelterpub.com/building/shelter.

# 5

## Bringing Your Environment to Life

In chapter 1 ("The Power of Immersion in Historical Environments"), I argued that the most engaging and memorable historical environments in museums involve—among other qualities—a cohesive, unified narrative. You have now reached the critical point in which you will be creating the narrative, or story, upon which your environment is based. It may be the hardest thing you have done so far. Why? Because most of us were not trained to think like storytellers. As museum scholar Daniel Spock explains, "In history class, we got good grades for presenting well-reasoned arguments supported by facts and generalized to larger societal trends over time."[1] Stories, on the other hand, do not start with facts. As Spock remarks, they more often begin at an intimate, personal level. They:

> tend to heighten the unique traits and foibles of each character and, more often than histories, they get expressed in the first and second person voice. This intimate view proves very accessible to those who otherwise claim to have little interest in history.[2]

Stories have numerous other advantages. They help us make sense of the world. They teach us what is possible. They let us know that others have struggled before us. They encourage us to empathize with people of other times and cultures while helping us to understand, remember, and share our own experiences. Finally, because stories have the ability to touch us on a deep emotional level, they provide a fundamental key to learning and problem solving.[3]

In this chapter, you will learn to harness the powerful medium of story to engage visitors on a variety of levels. This begins by creating a backstory—a classic literary device that explains a character's history, personality, and perspective. Writing a backstory, drawn from your conceptual framework and historical research, ensures that people are not only a presence in your environment but also that they are believable, historically plausible, and emotionally compelling. With a backstory in hand, you can then take the next steps—determining the interpretive strategy and developing the furnishings plan that will bring your story to life.

## DEVELOPING A BACKSTORY

### What Is a Backstory?

A backstory is a literary device with which you are probably all familiar.[4] Compelling stories are built upon the premise that a character's past sets up and explains who the character is in the present. The backstory involves everything that happened before the story began; it is the unseen history that informs all of a character's current decisions and reactions. Through the use of backstory, the characters and their world become more realistic. When we know the details of the character's background, we become more invested in the story.

Sometimes, the backstory can be overt, as in author J. R. R. Tolkien's detailed explanations of Middle Earth and its inhabitants in his *Lord of the Rings* trilogy through lengthy descriptions of family trees, geography, and history. At other times, the backstory is more subtle, as in author J. K. Rowling's slow reveal of Harry Potter's background through situations and dialogue over the course of seven books.

Often, a backstory describes a single character or a group of characters. But it can also elucidate a situation in which characters are present. For example, as mentioned in chapter 2, Walt Disney Imagineers have become particularly adept at their use of backstories to develop attractions, settings, and experiences at Disney theme parks.[5] Although my examples thus far have been drawn primarily from the realm of fiction, a backstory can be equally applicable to fleshing out the background relating to real people and situations.[6]

### The Use of Backstory in Museums

Within the museum context, conceptual framework and historical research play important roles in helping to shape the content of a character or situational backstory. The idea of character development, which has long played a crucial role in both museum theater and first-person role-playing interpretation, embodies the notion of backstory. From these disciplines, we can glean insightful strategies into the development of backstories for historical environments.

In his article "Theater 101 for Historical Interpretation," museum theater specialist Dale Jones advises that characters in dramatic programs should ideally possess a sense of "aliveness," a believable personality, a rational logic to the way they react and respond to different people and situations.[7] In developing a character, Jones explains, one should ask questions such as What is the major obstacle or success the character faces in the story or event that you are relating? How does the character react to this? Does the character have any second thoughts about his or her actions? Knowing the answers to questions like these helps make the character seem more real. When this sense of "aliveness" is successfully achieved through the technique of character development, the audience becomes more willing to suspend disbelief and can better relate to and sympathize with the characters.

As much as possible, theatrical performances in history museums are based upon historical research and involve real history, issues, and context. Although some aspects of character development must be, by necessity, a judgment call, these performances aim to be "historically plausible" or a reasonable extrapolation of what might have happened.[8] This is equally true when developing character backstories for a historical environment.

In her book *Past into Present: Effective Techniques for First-Person Historical Interpretation*, historical interpretation specialist Stacy Roth also describes strategies for developing believable characters.[9] All characters, Roth argues—whether they are factual, representative, or composite—need a history, a personality, and a perspective. To develop a character with depth and validity for first-person interpretation, Roth proposes a framework based upon a list of specific topics that she groups into five spheres of knowledge:

- Personal (for example, birthplace and date, family relationships, personal habits and belongings, and social skills and traits).
- Local (what the character shares with others, including social class, religious customs, dress, foodways, and material culture).
- Occupational/domestic (involving skills and related tools, processes, wages, and skill-based terminology).
- Stational (that is, one's station in life as well as characteristics and habits related to social class).
- Worldly (including awareness of global phenomena, world events, well-known figures, and world geography and economy).[10]

Knowing the character's place and stance in relation to these spheres, Roth argues, convinces visitors they are conversing with a believable person of the past. Like museum theater, developing characters for first-person historic interpretation should depend, as much as possible, upon documentary evidence.

Historic house specialist Nancy Bryk brings the concept of character development directly into the historic house environment.[11] Bryk argues that a historic house interior should visually communicate significant messages about the inhabitants who lived there. For these interiors to be believable, they must incorporate characters that possess believable personalities, motivations, and mindsets. Similar to Roth's spheres of knowledge, Bryk suggests listing out and addressing a series of questions for the characters to be portrayed there. Again, drawing as much as possible from the historical research, these questions include the following:

- Cultural expectations (such as, whether the characters followed the tenets of prescriptive literature regarding room decoration and use; their self-consciousness about presentation of self; and their attitudes toward using items that have faded from popularity).
- Family relationships (including parental permission for children to explore and experiment as well as parental encouragement of intellectual discourse).
- Adventure and travel (involving characters' tendency to be provincial or cosmopolitan; whether the characters possess an adventurous nature; and the effect of travel and adventure on the characters).
- Other relationships (for example, important relationships in forging the characters' attitudes; experiences—either loving and supportive or challenging and adversarial—with other family members and with people not part of the family).
- Activities (important activities in the characters' lives as well as how these help reveal the uniqueness of the characters).
- Events or traumas (including events—local, national, or both—that were pivotal to the maturation or careers of the characters).[12]

## Creating Backstory Questions

To write a backstory, begin by determining what/whom your backstory is about: a single individual; a composite group of characters; or a place, situation, or event. The individuals might be actual people or representative characters based upon real people. You can create separate backstories for different people if you want to consider each character individually. Then, complete a character development worksheet containing a list of questions and your responses to those questions. The questions you create can draw from the helpful lists described above by Jones, Roth, and Bryk, but they should be geared to your own project's needs and goals. Furthermore, your responses to these questions should incorporate your historical research. How do you know you have asked the "correct" backstory questions, let alone answered them appropriately? You will have to weigh what you know with what you surmise, then make your best judgment. Remember that this is primarily a planning tool—or, as the Disney Imagineers call it, a design aid.

## REAL-LIFE EXAMPLE: QUESTIONS FOR THE "BACK-TO-THE-LAND" COMMUNE BACKSTORY[13]

Since this recreated environment in the *Your Place in Time* exhibition was intended to focus on a representative group of commune dwellers, we needed to create a backstory that would lead to believable and emotionally engaging characters. To accomplish this, I worked with another museum staff member who had both lived in a communal environment like this one in the early 1970s and knew others who had lived that way as well. Together, we created a series of questions that covered as many aspects of the representative group's motivations for living in the commune and their lifestyle there as we could think of, including:

- Who lived here?
- Why did they come?
- What were their backgrounds, experiences, personalities, motivations?
- What were their expectations for living here?
- Who founded the commune?
- What was their motivation for founding it?
- How was it organized? How did it function from day to day?
- What kinds of tasks were expected of commune dwellers?

We then delved into a range of possible responses to each of these questions. This resulted in a composite backstory that represented a "community" of people who might have lived here, how their place might have been furnished and why, what they did on a daily basis, how they might have related to one another, and what their personalities, mindset, attitudes, and values were (see Figure 5.1).

**Figure 5.1.**  One of many evidences of the backstory that was created for the back-to-the-landers who might have lived in this 1973 commune environment in the *Your Place in Time* exhibition is a shelf lined with the types of books that various individuals might have owned.
Photo by Deborah Berk

## Writing the Backstory

The next step in writing a backstory is what differentiates it from a straight biography. Creating a backstory involves knowing and incorporating story elements. Numerous books, articles, and websites describe standard story elements in many different ways.[14] But they generally all agree that stories contain these key commonalities:

1. A story, any story, is usually about someone struggling or striving. Often involving inner turmoil or a confrontation with people who have differing perspectives or viewpoints, this implies that the main character is active. In writing your backstory, you should ask: What does the character want? Why does he or she want that? How might he or she work to get that?
2. People (aka "characters") are the central key to good stories. They must come alive, live and breathe in believable ways, take charge of their own stories. They must have a motive for making decisions, for dealing with

the struggle, which moves beyond stereotype. Their background, personality, values, and mindset all play into these motives. The more you know about your character—how he or she feels about, reacts to, and responds to things—the more fully you can bring that character to life. Whether the characters in your environment *are* real people or are representative of a place and time, they should *act* like real people—surprise us, convince us, act in particular and precise ways (i.e., "in character"). In writing your backstory, you should ask: What are the character traits that set this person/these people apart? What makes them tick? What in their history provides a key to understanding their motives?

3.  A story has a plot that unfolds as a sequence of actions or series of events over time. It involves an attempt to solve a problem and bring about some resolution, or at least closure, in the end. In writing your backstory, you should ask: What action is occurring? How does it evolve and change over time? How does it bring the character(s) to some resolution or closure?

4.  A story's setting should be rich in visual imagery and details. It both provides a backdrop to the backstory and reinforces it wherever possible. The setting conveys messages (overt or subtle) about the characters. For a historical environment the setting is, of course, a key asset.

5.  A story has a theme, a main point that ties it together. In writing your backstory, you should ask: How is the character's problem resolved? What is learned? How does the character grow? Can we take away some insight, some truth, from this?

The key to creating a powerful backstory is your ability to bring your characters to life through the use of these story elements: strong characters struggling or striving to achieve something or solve a problem, a plot or sequence of actions that moves the characters toward resolution, and a theme that ties it all together. The characters may not reach resolution, but there should be a lesson learned. It should have an emotional quality, revealing and eliciting such feelings as uncertainty, surprise, anticipation, or sadness. At all times, it revolves around people—their motivations, their personalities, their values, and their mindset. As backstory expert Larry Fisher explains:

> The most important part of a backstory is that you look for a sense of purpose to the story. You create a reason for the moments in time you're depicting. The next step is to look at your notes and see what ideas percolate. To do that, you have to know the elements of a good story: character development, context, inquiry or conflict or emotional elements (not only between characters but between the characters and the audience). You look for tension, curiosity. You look at how guests might put themselves in the shoes of those characters and feel the emotions themselves.[15]

**CHECKLIST 5.1.**
**Writing a Backstory**

1. Determine the subject (character, composite group of characters, or situation) of your backstory.
2. Complete a character development worksheet with a list of questions. The suggestions in this chapter can provide a jumping-off point for creating these questions, but they should be customized to your own project's needs and goals.
3. Write your responses to the questions, incorporating your historical research and suppositions based upon that research.
4. Consider the story elements described in this chapter (struggle, characters, plot, setting, theme).
5. Write the narrative.
6. Edit it until it is concise, cohesive, and compelling.
7. Repeat with other characters and/or subjects if desired.

## REAL-LIFE EXAMPLE: EXCERPT FROM THE BACKSTORY FOR "J. R. JONES, WATERFORD, MICHIGAN STOREKEEPER," WRITTEN FOR THE J. R. JONES GENERAL STORE[16]

It took only a little bit of capital but a lot of business ingenuity and risk taking to run a general store in the late 1800s. Because of the great financial risks involved, many storekeepers went out of business, and stores changed hands often. This general store was one such store. Built in the village of Waterford, Michigan, about 1856, it changed hands at least nine times before being purchased by Henry Ford in 1927. J. R. Jones, the store's proprietor between 1882 and 1888, was like many other storekeepers of his time—low on funds but high on ambition and filled with the dream of prosperity just around the corner.

Jimmie (as J. R. was called into adulthood) must have fancied himself quite a salesman when he clerked at his brother's store while still in his teens. By the time he was twenty, he was already in charge of operating T. G. Richardson's store in Waterford (about twelve miles southeast of Holly, on the main rail line to Pontiac). And he must have been pretty good at that. A newspaper account of the time reports that "Mr. James Jones, the accomplished 'how many yards ma'am,' from Holly has charge of Richardson's store here and is well liked."

## YOUR INTERPRETIVE STRATEGY

Determining the interpretive strategy for your historical environment—that is, the right mixture of interpretive techniques, programs, offerings, and auxiliary products—is key to both helping get your message(s) across and creating an experience that is engaging and memorable to your visitors. You may refine and adjust this later as a result of changing institutional plans, priorities, and resources. But at this point, the interpretive strategy will help you flesh out your furnishings plan, refine your budget, and determine your implementation plan.

According to Stephen Bitgood's findings (as described in chapter 1), immersion experiences have a high potential to entice, attract, and capture attention. The interest is there; the curiosity is piqued. The goal in developing an interpretive strategy for these environments is to ensure that visitors' initial interest and curiosity will turn into longer periods of attention by delivering upon perceived value. Interpretive techniques for historical environments should, like the components of any engaging visitor-focused experience, encourage discovery and exploration while avoiding confusion, boredom, overload, and fatigue.

The following is a list of interpretive techniques to consider for your historical environment. Each of these comes with strengths and weaknesses. I have not differentiated between interpretive techniques within museum exhibitions and those in historic structures. Such techniques as interpretive labels can be as effective in historic structures and sites as in exhibitions; conversely, live interpreters, theatrical programs, and guided tours can enhance museum exhibitions as effectively as they can historic structures and sites (see Table 5.1).

Table 5.1.   Interpretive Techniques: Strengths and Weaknesses

| Interpretive Technique | Strengths | Weaknesses |
|---|---|---|
| Multisensory Enhancements | Can heighten impact in small but effective ways | Need consideration of sensory sensitivities; will likely need adjustment and monitoring |
| Interpretive Labels | Offer a relatively cost-effective way of conveying intended messages | Can be too didactic; can break with immersive quality of environment; may need monitoring and replacement if heavily used; any media will need maintaining and updating |

*(continued)*

**Table 5.1.  Continued**

| Interpretive Technique | Strengths | Weaknesses |
|---|---|---|
| Live Interpretation/ Guided Tours | Presence of people can enhance immersive quality of environment; experience can be adjusted to different visitors | Can be repetitive, fixed, and passive; extra resources are needed to equip, staff, and train; any media will need maintaining and updating |
| Self-Guided Experiences | Can be relatively inexpensive; visitors can customize their own experience | Little control over what visitors are getting out of the experience; will likely need physical barriers, which break with immersive quality of environment; any technology will need maintaining and updating |
| Interactives | Engaging and memorable for visitors; can enhance feeling of immersion as visitors "step in shoes" of people who might have inhabited that space | If developed as activity for activity's sake, can detract from environment and intended messages; need prototyping and monitoring; might need additional adjustment and replacement; additional staffing might be needed; technology-based interactives will need updating |
| Theatrical Performances | Add to immersive quality because they involve people, storytelling, and emotion; can communicate complex aspects of human behavior | Resource intensive; require special expertise and ongoing monitoring |

## Multisensory Enhancements

According to Bitgood's studies described in chapter 1, multisensory stimulation seems particularly important in creating the feeling of immersion. Indeed, enhancing sensory elements in a historical environment—such as lighting, sound, and smell—can greatly heighten its impact.[17] At a living history site, chances are that rich, multisensory experiences involving touch, smell, and even taste may already be incorporated into the experience. Through creative planning, multisensory elements can be added to enhance the immersive nature of other environments as well.

## Interpretive Labels

In her book *Exhibit Labels: An Interpretive Approach*, Beverly Serrell defines an interpretive label as "any label that serves to explain, guide, question, inform, or provoke—in a way that invites active participation by the reader."[18] In place of a typical didactic label, you might consider going in a more story-based direction for the text of your interpretive label(s). Just as historical environments tell stories, so might your label text incorporate story elements. How might you create a scenario for your environment and tell it in the form of a story? How might you bring the backstory to life through a label? How might you create and use "environmental graphics" that look and feel like they came from the time and place of your environment, to help enhance and reinforce the story (see Figure 5.2)?

**Figure 5.2.** This "environmental graphic"—written in nineteenth-century script and based upon an actual announcement in a newspaper of the era—is tacked up on the back wall of the J. R. Jones Store, along with several advertisements and other community notices.

Photo by Deborah Berk

## Live Interpreters and Guided Tours

Many historic structures and sites are staffed with live interpreters, using forms of interpretation commonly referred to as third person, first person, and role-playing.[19] Guided tours are especially common in historic houses and are occasionally offered across entire historic sites and within museum exhibitions.[20] Audio and video can be added to enhance guided tours.

## Self-Guided Experiences

Unstaffed historic structures and exhibitions can be supplemented not only by interpretive labels but also by written brochures, downloadable maps and guides, digital kiosks containing deeper information, and mobile apps that describe the main points of each stop. These can all be effective vehicles for conveying interpretive themes, research findings, and backstory—especially if they are visually appealing, well written, and easy to follow. Scripted audio can add to the immersive quality, especially if it is written in a narrative format.

## Interactives

Interactives can greatly enhance the experience within a historical environment. One category of interactives is low-tech, hands-on activities that are especially engaging to families and younger audiences.[21] Whether within the context of a historic structure or site, or planned as part of an exhibition environment, these activities should always reinforce, not detract from, the experience. Technology-based interactives—such as motion-based technology and augmented reality—can help reinforce the story of your environment, attract new audiences, and potentially extend the experience beyond the museum after the visit. But keep in mind that technology changes quickly and will be more costly to implement, monitor, and update.

## Theatrical Performances

Theatrical performances use trained actors in a scripted dramatic presentation.[22] With their richly textured settings, historical environments can serve as perfect backdrops to the staging of theatrical performances. Because of theater's traditional focus on storytelling and emotion, visitors are easily drawn in, feel that they are being entertained rather than talked at, and are willing to suspend disbelief as they become participants themselves in this imagined world. Moreover, studies have shown that visitors not only enjoy these performances but see meaning and relevance in the issues being presented, often more clearly than through the more traditional methods of presenting historical information (see Figure 5.3).

**Figure 5.3.** The popular theatrical performance, "The Disagreeable Customer"—about an uppity doctor's wife from Detroit who reluctantly shops at the J. R. Jones Store—explores tensions between city and country dwellers at that time.
Photo by Elaine Kaiser

## Public and Educational Programs

In addition to interpretive techniques and components that can enhance visitor interaction and engagement within an immersive space, more intensive and longer-term programming—for both general and special audiences—should also be considered and can begin to be planned at this time.[23]

The daily interpretation of historical environments can be augmented through enhanced programming during special events or special themed weekends. This involves additional planning, training, and implementation. But, when planned to closely dovetail with the environment's interpretive themes, research findings, and backstory, these can be extremely effective, engaging, and memorable. They often allow for deeper treatment of a part of the story; provide a more in-depth, meaningful experience for specific target audiences; and allow the environment to take on a different quality or be highlighted in a different way than its regular daily use and appearance (see Figures 5.3 and 6.4).

The objects and stories of historical environments have rich potential for both school-age audiences (preschool, K–12, homeschool, after school, and university) and their teachers. These should align with curriculum goals established by the teachers working in concert with museum educators. They also can lend themselves to activities, tours, and storytelling for scout groups, special classes, summer camps, and community outreach programs.

## Offerings for Audiences with Special Needs

Today, many museums are going beyond the legal obligations of ADA (the Americans with Disabilities Act, passed in 1990) to provide opportunities and educational offerings for people of all abilities—including people who are blind or have low vision, are deaf or hard of hearing, or have developmental or cognitive disabilities (e.g., autism and dementia).[24] Historical environments offer many opportunities for these audiences to engage with the stories, and the interpretive techniques you choose can be geared toward meeting their needs, cognitive abilities, and interests. This can involve multiple modes of presenting and receiving information, such as tactile maps and models, audio description to complement visual and tactile experiences, and large-print versions of interpretive labels.

In addition, tour offerings and interpretive programs can include touchable objects (or reproductions), descriptive language that advances an interpretive story for visitors who are blind or have low vision, sign language interpretation for visitors who are deaf or hard of hearing, and inquiry- and discussion-based programs for people with dementia and their care partners, with facilitators asking questions that foster conversation and spark memories among participants (see Figure 6.5).

## Auxiliary Interpretive Products

As mentioned in chapter 1, Bitgood's studies have suggested that immersion experiences are among the more memorable aspects of a museum visit. These memories can be transformed into deeply meaningful aspects of people's lives, turn into family stories that are recounted time and time again, and lead to longer-term interest and learning. They might inspire visitors to dig deeper into a topic, through reading and travel, or lead to a call to action to take a stand, effect societal change, or pursue a path in their own personal lives. For these reasons, it is worth providing opportunities to extend that personal encounter, through such auxiliary products as digital content on web sites; brochures, publications, or other printed material; merchandise and souvenirs; and related post-visit curriculum materials.

## YOUR FURNISHINGS PLAN

With an initial interpretive strategy in hand, you can now focus on your furnishings plan. This plan documents in two dimensions what the three-dimensional environment will look like. It contains two key elements: a furnishings rationale and a detailed inventory.[25] The plan will likely be refined as you hone your list of available objects and reproductions, your interpretive strategy, your layout, and your final installation (see chapter 6).

## The Furnishings Rationale

For the first time, you are imagining in real terms what the concrete, physical space will look like. Perhaps at this point you are filled with dread. What if you made mistakes along the way? What if you missed something crucially important? The best advice I can give you is to be as disciplined and rigorous as possible, and document everything along the way. But, in the end, you will have to take some leaps of faith and have confidence in your ability to both analyze and imagine. As William Seale claims, "Almost every restored interior represents a combination of fact and supposition."[26] Similarly, Nancy Bryk encourages curators to apply "disciplined imagination" by combining knowledge of the time, place, and material culture with what is known or implied about the people who inhabited the space.[27]

I have found that the most advantageous way to both guide your own decisions about furnishings and to help you explain those decisions to others is to begin with a written rationale that describes the overall vision for your arrangement. Here are some examples:

## REAL-LIFE EXAMPLE: FURNISHINGS RATIONALE FOR McGUFFEY BIRTHPLACE[28]

Aligned with the interpretive themes, goals, and research findings, the plan for McGuffey Birthplace was to furnish it to the date span of 1800 to 1802—the period during which the McGuffey family resided there. As closely as possible, the furnishings of the home would reflect the needs and personalities of the adventurous and illiterate father Alexander, the educated and refined mother Anna, and their three young children (Jane, age 3; William, age 2; and Henry, an infant).

The placement of the furnishings would also reflect the family's Scots-Irish background: with the hearth as the focal point and a clear path leading to it from the front door; with Anna's things placed to the left of the hearth and Alexander's to the right; and with the bed and corner cupboard representing the most valuable items in the household. Cherished family items and dishes would be displayed in the cupboard (see Figure 5.4).

Historian Jennifer Ford's "toolkit" list of basic furnishings (chapter 4) served as a guide to determining the smaller furnishings and household items in the home, including: a work table; a few mismatched chairs; food

Figure 5.4. A loose rope barrier in the unstaffed McGuffey Birthplace subtly demarcates the visitor area from the furnished space. Scripted audio presentations in this building represent two alternating perspectives: William Holmes McGuffey's parents at the time of interpretation (1800–1802) and McGuffey himself as a grown man looking back.
Photo by the author

service equipment like bowls, mugs, plates, and spoons; food preparation equipment like a butter churn, iron pots, and a teakettle; and kegs and barrels for storing food.

## REAL-LIFE EXAMPLE: FURNISHINGS RATIONALE FOR J. R. JONES GENERAL STORE[29]

The rationale for furnishing this building was to simulate, as closely as possible, an actual working general merchandise store of the mid-1880s. It would be stocked in keeping with references we had found in the historical research that this store carried "groceries, dry goods, boots, shoes, &c." Another historical reference to this store as a "farmers' supply store" also led to our decision to include an array of agricultural products and a variety of other items intended to meet the needs of families living in the surrounding agricultural community. A stock of sporting goods, specifically documented to Jones's proprietorship, would be featured in the store as well, along with his desk and items like boots and shoes which were mentioned in his personal reminiscence when he visited the store in Greenfield Village in 1927 (see Figures 5.5 and 6.3). The idea of the "working store" implied that there would be quantities of the same objects and that they would need to appear as new and unused as possible (see Figures 5.6 and 6.1).

**Figure 5.5.  This front-window display of hunting, fishing, and baseball accoutrements in the J. R. Jones Store was created after newspaper documentation indicated that Jones had stocked a supply of sporting goods.**
Photo by Deborah Berk

## REAL-LIFE EXAMPLE: FURNISHINGS RATIONALE FOR 1973 "BACK-TO-THE-LAND" COMMUNE, *YOUR PLACE IN TIME* EXHIBITION[30]

Building upon the research findings and the backstory for this environment, this furnishings rationale involved a "community" of like-minded people who were seeking and experimenting with simpler, alternative ways of living. Clues to these lifestyle choices and attitudes would be apparent everywhere visitors looked in the space. Based upon images from the *Shelter* publication, the space would look as lived in as possible—furnished with used castoffs (e.g., cabinet, chairs, dishes); hand-crafted items (e.g., macramé plant holder, punched tin lanterns); earlier forms of technology (e.g., coal-burning stove, kerosene lamps, treadle sewing machine, candles); and cookbooks and cooking ingredients that indicated a rejection of processed mainstream foods (see Figure 4.5). Posters and notices would reference social and political views, while the choice of books would reflect various commune members' backgrounds, education, and interests (see Figures 1.4 and 5.1). A job list tacked to the refrigerator would indicate their attempts to work together in this communal living situation. The lamp and overhead lighting fixtures would be functional.

### The Furnishings Inventory

An item-by-item inventory of furnishings should follow your furnishings rationale, grouped by location and noting the following information:

- Whether the item is an artifact or reproduction.
- If the item is an artifact, along with its date, provenance, and accession number.
- If applicable, what objects you know were originally in this environment (this pertains particularly to historic structures) or were owned by the people whose stories are being told in this space.
- If a reproduction, its source and cost.
- If applicable, structural and setting details such as lighting fixtures, floor covering, window treatments, wall and ceiling treatments.
- Important visual references that support your decisions, with captions and identification numbers. If these references are not from your collections, cite your sources.[31]

You will likely refine this list several times as the project moves forward.

## PLANNING FOR PROPS AND REPRODUCTIONS

Whether called props or reproductions, these facsimiles of objects that were made and used in the past should be considered logical and important additions to the furnishings plan of a historical environment. In her article, "But They're Not Real! Rethinking the Use of Props in Historic House Museum Displays," Bethany Watkins Sugawara advises that "Used effectively, props can provide a vital link between the static objects of a past life and the visitor's understanding of what that life must have been like."[32] Props can draw the eye, lend interest and atmosphere, bring the past to life, and serve as excellent interpretive tools when real objects are lacking or are too rare or fragile to display. These can include such items as letters, sheet music, food, clothing, accessories—anything that adds a lived-in atmosphere to the environment and enhances the impression that real people might have inhabited this space.

Sometimes the term "reproduction" is used to specifically imply a custom-made object that simulates—as closely as possible—an original artifact that cannot be displayed because of its fragility, rarity, or expense. But the line between props and reproductions is often a gray one. Whatever term you use, it is always a good idea to have a plan in place for choosing, tracking, and maintaining these noncollection items. This includes determining:

- How you are defining the terms reproduction and prop.
- What criteria you are using to determine the need for such items.
- Who is responsible for choosing and acquiring them.
- How these will be documented, tracked, and moved.
- How these will be displayed (e.g., because these are not real artifacts, they can be affixed to a surface or modified in some way to keep them in place and intact).
- How these will be treated, repaired, or replaced if they wear out, break, or become missing.
- From what budget these will be purchased, maintained, and replaced.

It is best if props and reproductions are tracked within the same collections management system as real artifacts.[33] These records become crucial documents over time when items need to be replaced, questions arise about them, or staff members change (see Figure 5.6).

**Figure 5.6.** A special numbering system keeps track of both reproductions and historic artifacts at the J. R. Jones Store, on both the objects themselves and in the Museum's collections management database. Reproductions here include the custom-made tin, paper, and cardboard items and the modern off-the-shelf clothesline, brushes, and wooden spoons. The cast iron flatirons and ceramic bowl are historic artifacts.
Photo by Deborah Berk

## FORMATIVE EVALUATION

There might come a time during the creation of your historical environment—while writing the backstory, developing interpretive techniques, or creating the furnishings or reproductions plan—during which you want to check in with your community advisers and/or with visitors in a systematic way (called formative evaluation). This middle-of-the-process check can help you detect and isolate problems in the midst of planning or design, before a great deal of time, money, and effort has been spent. It can improve comprehension and clarity, enhancing visitor engagement with the story.

Formative evaluation can be highly useful, even if it is brief, narrowly focused, and involves a small sample of visitors.[34] Handmade mock-ups and small-scale prototypes can provide a reliable basis for predicting how the public will react to the final product. Once problems have been detected, corrections can be made and retested until the component achieves the desired results based upon stated goals and objectives. Keep in mind that it is difficult for visitors to picture a space or experience from a drawing or floor plan. And, at this stage, you will likely have little actual physical environment to show them or take them through.

Prototyping interpretive techniques and components at this point is also strongly recommended, especially hands-on activities, technology-based interactives, and self-guided written materials. Do these hold up with use? Do visitors understand how to use them? Do they enjoy using them? Do they understand the point you are trying to get across?

---

**CHECKLIST 5.2.**
**The Program Plan**

Like the project brief described in chapter 3 ("Framing Your Project") and the research report described in chapter 4 ("Your Research Methodology"), the program plan puts all of your hard work described in this chapter into a written document for current and future reference. It can also serve as a milestone review document at this point. The program plan includes:

- The backstory(ies)
- The interpretive strategy
  - Interpretive intent
  - Interpretive techniques
  - Public and educational programs
  - Offerings for audiences with special needs
  - Auxiliary interpretive products
- The furnishings plan
  - The furnishings rationale
  - A detailed inventory of furnishings, calling out artifacts and repro-ductions
  - Preliminary arrangement of the furnishings
  - Lighting, floor, wall, and window treatments
  - Related images and bibliographic citations
- Mid-process check with community advisers and/or formative visitor evaluation
- Implementation plan, which might include:
  - Conservation plan for collections
  - Artifact needs
  - Reproductions plan
- Refined budget and schedule

## LOOKING AHEAD

This chapter described the steps of bringing your historical environment to life through the power of story. It begins with developing a backstory, which lays the foundation for the next steps—determining the interpretive strategy and creating the furnishings plan that will convey that story. A mid-process check—through formative evaluation and/or checking back with your community advisers—helps confirm that your ideas thus far are sound. Now, you are ready to put it all together—writing a visitor experience walkthrough, determining a layout and, ultimately, stepping into the exciting (and sometimes scary) world of actually creating the environment and seeing it "come alive" in a three-dimensional space. But, even then, you're not finished. The final steps—documentation, summative evaluation, and monitoring and adjustment—will ensure that your environment has maximum appeal and lasting impact.

## NOTES

1. Daniel Spock, "A Practical Guide to Personal Connectivity," *History News* 63, no. 4 (Autumn 2008): 14.

2. Ibid., 15.

3. These ideas were inspired by Marion Dune Bauer, *What's Your Story? A Young Person's Guide to Writing Fiction* (New York: Clarion Books, 1992), ix; Best Practice Analysis, "America on the Move" Front-End Study, implemented by Institute for Learning Innovation, 11–27 (unpublished manuscript, September 2000); and Dale Jones, "Personal Connections and the Great Cosmic Soup," *History News* 63, no. 2 (Spring 2008): 16. For more on the advantages of stories, see Leslie Bedford, "Storytelling: The Real Work of Museums," *Curator* 44, no. 1 (January 2001): 27–34.

4. For more on backstory as a literary device, see Bauer, *What's Your Story?*, 20–21; Lisa Cron, *Wired for Story: The Writer's Guide to Using Brain Science to Hook Readers from the Very First Sentence* (Berkeley, CA: Ten Speed Press, 2012), 211; K. M. Weiland, "Backstory: The Importance of What Isn't Told," Helping Writers Become Authors website, August 16, 2009, accessed April 28, 2018, https://www.helpingwritersbecomeauthors.com/backstory-importance-of-what-isnt-told/; and Eleanor Henderson, "I Wasn't Born Yesterday: The Beauty of the Backstory," Poets & Writers website, August 31, 2013, accessed April 28, 2018, https://www.pw.org/content/i_wasnt_born_yesterday_the_beauty_of_backstory.

5. The Imagineers, *Walt Disney Imagineering: A Behind the Dreams Look at Making the Magic Real* (New York: Hyperion, 1996), 42–43. Several examples of backstories developed for Disney theme parks are also included here.

6. Narrative, or creative, nonfiction provides a useful model for exploring this concept further. Narrative nonfiction writers begin with well-researched historical

information about their topics. Then, they apply story elements, like strong character portrayals, a dramatic unfolding of events, descriptive settings, and active verbs, to make the reading experience vivid, emotionally compelling, and enjoyable. Excellent examples of narrative nonfiction that incorporate these elements include Timothy Egan's *The Worst Hard Time: The Untold Story of Those Who Survived the Great American Dust Bowl* (Boston: Houghton Mifflin Co., 2006); David Laskin's *The Children's Blizzard* (New York: HarperPerennial, 2005); and Nathaniel Philbrick's *In the Heart of the Sea: The Tragedy of the Whaleship* Essex (Penguin Books, 2001). For more on this type of writing, see Theodore A. Rees Cheney, *Writing Creative Nonfiction: Fiction Techniques for Crafting Great Nonfiction* (Berkeley, CA: Ten Speed Press, 2001).

7. Dale Jones, "Theater 101 for Historical Interpretation," *History News* 59, no. 3 (Summer 2004): Technical Leaflet #227, 3.

8. Ibid., 2.

9. Stacy F. Roth, *Past into Present: Effective Techniques for First-Person Historical Interpretation* (Chapel Hill: University of North Carolina Press, 1998): 57–63.

10. For an even more detailed list in Roth's book, see Appendix 2: "The Ultimate Character Development List: A Guide for the Gung-ho Interpreter," 186–93.

11. Nancy E. Villa Bryk, "'I Wish You Could Take a Peak at Us in the Present Moment': Infusing the Historic House with Characters and Activity," in *Interpreting Historic House Museums*, ed. Jessica Foy Donnelly (Walnut Creek, CA: AltaMira Press, a Division of Rowman & Littlefield, 2002): 144–67.

12. For more fleshed-out questions, see the section in Bryk's essay on "Connecting the Domestic Environment to Its Characters," 152–55.

13. Unpublished manuscripts: "The Reason Why We're Here" (n.d., ca. 1999); "Backstory for Commune in *Your Place in Time* Exhibition, Sample Questions" (27 March 2007), Donna Braden Papers, Benson Ford Research Center, The Henry Ford, Dearborn, MI (hereafter cited as Braden Papers).

14. For more on story elements, see Bauer, *What's Your Story?*; LaPlante, *The Making of a Story*; and Thomas R. Arp and Greg Johnson, *Perrine's Story and Structure: An Introduction to Fiction*, 12th ed. (Boston: Wadsworth Cengage Learning, 2009). Also, see the free online resource, "Pixar in a Box: The Art of Storytelling," a collaboration between Pixar Animation Studios and Khan Academy that offers an interactive exploration of the storytelling process at Pixar, accessed July 14, 2018, https://www.khanacademy.org/partner-content/pixar/storytelling.

15. Larry Fisher, in-person interview, May 11, 2018. Larry Fisher, currently executive director of the NHRA Motorsports Museum, Pomona, California, is a designer, experience developer, and one-time Walt Disney Imagineer who was instrumental in envisioning the *Your Place in Time* exhibition at Henry Ford Museum of American Innovation.

16. "The J. R. Jones General Store in Greenfield Village, Program Plan," Donna R. Braden and Blake D. Hayes (unpublished manuscript, 15 September 1992), Braden Papers.

17. For more on multisensory enhancements as an exhibition technique, see section entitled "Gestalt – Sensory Perception Forming a Whole," in Polly McKenna-Cress

and Janet Kamien, *Creating Exhibitions: Collaboration in the Planning, Development, and Design of Innovative Experiences* (Hoboken, NJ: John Wiley and Sons, 2013), 153–61; and section entitled "Lighting the Way," in Kathleen McLean, *Planning for People in Museum Exhibitions* (Washington, DC: The Association of Science-Technology Centers, 1993), 141–49.

18. Beverly Serrell, *Exhibit Labels: An Interpretive Approach*, 2nd ed. (Lanham, MD: Rowman & Littlefield, 2015), 19. Additional studies of visitors and label reading include Bitgood, *Engaging the Visitor*, 50–111; McLean, *Planning for People in Museum Exhibitions*, 103–14; Chandler G. Screven, "Motivating Visitors to Read Labels," *Text in the Exhibition Medium*, ed. Andrée Blais (Quebec City: La Société des Musées Québécois and Musée de la Civilisation, 1994), 97–132; Judy Rand, Ann Grimes, Robert Kiihne, and Sarah Watkins, "Families First! Rethinking Exhibits to Engage All Ages," *History News* 64, no. 1 (Winter 2009): Technical Leaflet #245; Judy Rand, "Write and Design with the Family in Mind," *Connecting Kids to History with Museum Exhibitions*, ed. D. Lynn McRainey and John Russick (Walnut Creek, CA: Left Coast Press, Inc., 2010), 257–84; and Judy Rand, "Less Is More. And More Is Less," *Exhibition: A Journal of Exhibition Theory & Practice for Museum Professionals* 32, no. 1 (Spring 2016): 36–41. This article is also available online at https://static1.squarespace.com/static/58fa260a725e25c4f30020f3/t/594d16c51b631be4c390c593/1498224358446/11_Exhibition_LessIsMore.pdf.

19. For a good description of the similarities and differences between these forms of interpretation, see Roth, *Past into Present*, 11–13. According to Roth, third-person interpreters—often dressed in period attire—describe, demonstrate, illustrate, and compare their subjects in ways that effectively communicate their meaning to visitors. But they refer to the past as past. In first-person and role-playing interpretation, interpreters recreate daily activities, thoughts, and behavior of real (or composite) historical people. They behave in a fashion that evokes, as closely as possible, the behavior, customs, beliefs, perspectives, and practices of the past people they represent. In living history environments, interpreters employ a combination of discourse, demonstration, and interaction within a historical or simulated environment. For numerous best-practice examples relating to these varying forms of interpretation, refer to the ALHFAM (Association for Living History, Farm and Agricultural Museums) online index of articles from the Proceedings of Annual Meetings at http://www.alhfam.org/Proceedings-Index.

20. Much has been written about developing and implementing tours as well as about hiring and training staff. See, for example, Levy, Lloyd, and Schreiber, *Great Tours!*; Barbara Abramoff Levy, "Historic House Tours That Succeed: Choosing the Best Tour Approach," in *Interpreting Historic House Museums*, ed. Jessica Foy Donnelly (Lanham, MD: AltaMira Press, a Division of Rowman & Littlefield, 2002), 192–209; Sandra Mackenzie Lloyd, "Creating Memorable Visits: How to Develop and Implement Theme-Based Tours," in *Interpreting Historic House Museums*, 210–30 (AltaMira Press, 2002); Margaret Piatt, "Engaging Visitors through Effective Communication, in *Interpreting Historic House Museums*, 231–50; Alison L. Grinder and E. Sue McCoy, *The Good Guide: A Sourcebook for Interpreters, Docents, and*

*Tour Guides* (Scottsdale, AZ: Ironwood Press, 1985); and *The Docent Handbook* (Berkeley, CA: National Docent Symposium Council, 2001).

21. Sources that describe interactives as interpretive techniques include Timothy Glines and David Grabitske, "Telling the Story: Better Interpretation at Small Historical Organizations," *History News* 58, no. 2 (Spring 2003): Technical Leaflet #222, 5; McKenna-Cress and Kamien, *Creating Exhibitions*, 168–69; Bitgood, *Engaging the Visitor*, 115–45; and McLean, *Planning for People in Exhibitions*, 92–102.

22. Helpful sources that describe theatrical performance as an interpretive technique include Jones, "Theater 101"; Dale Jones, "Living History in the City," *History News* 50, no. 3 (Summer 1995): 10–13; and Catherine Hughes, *Museum Theatre: Communicating with Visitors through Drama* (Portsmouth, NH: Heinemann, 1998).

23. See Jamie Credle, "Endless Possibilities: Historic House Museum Programs That Make Educators Sing," in *Interpreting Historic House Museums*, ed. Jessica Foy Donnelly, 269–92 (Lanham, MD: AltaMira Press, 2002).

24. This topic is succinctly described in Caroline Braden's article, "Welcoming All Visitors: Museums, Accessibility, and Visitors with Disabilities," *University of Michigan Working Papers in Museum Studies*, Number 12 (2016), 3–15, accessed June 23, 2018, http://ummsp.rackham.umich.edu/wp-content/uploads/2016/10/Braden-working-paper-FINAL-pdf.pdf. See also Michele Hartley, "Shifting the Conversation: Improving Access with Universal Design," *N.A.M.E. Exhibitionist* 34, no. 2 (Fall 2015): 42; the issue on "Museums and Accessibility," *Museum* 94, no. 5 (September/October 2015); the issue on "Creating an Inclusive Experience: Exhibitions and Universal Design," *N.A.M.E. Exhibitionist* 34, no. 2 (Fall 2015); and McKenna-Cress and Kamien, *Creating Exhibitions*, 180–83.

25. Furnishings plans for historic structures and historic houses can be extensive and extremely detailed, incorporating historic structure analysis, an interpretive plan, historical research, and operational information. Sources that describe different components of furnishings plans include Seale, *Recreating the Historic House Interior*; Katz-Hyman and Woodcock, "The Basics of Writing Furnishings Plans," *Proceedings of the 2000 Conference and Annual Meeting, Mystic, Connecticut*, ed. Ron Kley and Jane Radcliffe, vol. XXIII (North Bloomfield, OH: The Association for Living History, Farm and Agricultural Museums, 2001): 158–62; Bradley Brooks, "The Historic House Furnishings Plan," in *Interpreting Historic House Museums*, 128–43; Marianna Curling, "How to Write a Furnishing Plan," *History News* 57, no. 2 (Spring 2002): Technical Leaflet #218; and "Guidelines for Preparing Historic Furnishings Reports," National Park Service Harpers Ferry Center, accessed March 21, 2018, https://www.nps.gov/hfc/products/furnish/furnish-plan-hfr-guide.cfm.

26. Seale, *Recreating the Historic House Interior*, 16.

27. Bryk, "'I Wish You Could Take a Peak at Us in the Present Moment,'" 163.

28. This draws from the following unpublished manuscripts: "Conceptual Overview, McGuffey Birthplace & School, Homes Programs" (29 January 2003); "McGuffey Birthplace Furnishing Plan" (10 April 2003, 29 April 2003, 5 May 2003); and "William Holmes McGuffey Historic Presenter Training Manual" (2003), Braden Papers.

29. From "The J. R. Jones General Store in Greenfield Village, Program Plan" (unpublished manuscript, 1992), Braden Papers.

30. Lloyd Kahn and Bob Easton, *Shelter* (Bolinas, CA: Shelter Publications, 1973); "A Guide to Our Place" and "Credits" [Back-to-the-Land Flipbook text] (unpublished manuscript, 1999); "Back to the Land Inventory" (unpublished manuscript, n.d., ca. 1999), Braden Papers.

31. Other books and articles that reference and describe furnishings inventories include Seale, *Recreating the Historic House Interior*; Bryk, "'I Wish You Could Take a Peak at Us in the Present Moment'"; Katz-Hyman and Woodcock, "The Basics of Writing Furnishings Plans"; and "Guidelines for Preparing Historic Furnishings Reports," National Park Service Harpers Ferry Center.

32. Bethany Watkins Sugawara, "But They're Not Real! Rethinking the Use of Props in Historic House Museum Displays," *History News* 58, no. 4 (August 2003), 20.

33. Some museums assign props and reproductions to a separate Study, Education, or Hands-on Collection. These items are specifically designated for use and considered expendable within the context of educational programs in the museum. At The Henry Ford, props and reproductions are tracked within the regular collections management system, which helps manage inventories and ensures that there is a record of where they were purchased or made.

34. Helpful published works on formative evaluation include *Try It! Improving Exhibits through Formative Evaluation*, ed. Sam Taylor and Beverly Serrell (Washington, DC: Association of Science-Technology Centers, 1992); *Introduction to Museum Evaluation*, ed. Minda Borun and Randi Korn (Washington, DC: American Association of Museums, 1999); Jill Stein, Marianna Adams, and Jessica Luke, "Thinking Evaluatively: A Practical Guide to Integrating the Visitor Voice," *History News* 62, no. 2 (Spring 2007): Technical Leaflet #238; Rand, Kihne, and Watkins, "Families First! Rethinking Exhibits to Engage All Ages"; Donna R. Braden, "Taste-Testing the Visitor Experience," *Proceedings of the 2013 Conference and Annual Meeting, Hale Farm & Village, Akron, Ohio*, ed. Debra A. Reid, vol. XXXVI (North Bloomfield, OH: The Association for Living History, Farm and Agricultural Museums, 2014): 197–211; and McKenna-Cress and Kamien, *Creating Exhibitions*, 124, 244–50.

# At Last! Creating Your Environment

This chapter leads you through the final steps of creating your historical environment. From the work you accomplished in chapter 5—writing a back-story, developing an interpretive strategy, and creating a furnishings plan, you will next capture in writing how you imagine your visitors will experience the environment. It is not unusual that this exercise might lead to your needing to make refinements in your interpretive strategy and furnishings plan. Next, you will translate the details of that narrative into a visual layout. Finally, you will bring your environment to life with the actual installation. If staff members are involved in the interpretation of the environment, you will want to communicate your vision to them through a formal training and a written manual so they can, in turn, translate that vision for visitors. Post-opening evaluation and ongoing attention to maintenance and refinement will ensure that your environment has maximum impact and lasting value.

## THE VISITOR EXPERIENCE WALKTHROUGH

After developing your interpretive strategy and completing your furnishings rationale and inventory (chapter 5), you will next go through the process of writing a visitor experience walkthrough. In this written narrative you imagine that you are an actual visitor experiencing the space.[1]

### Storyboard Origins

The visitor experience walkthrough hearkens back to the venerable idea of the storyboard, credited to Webb Smith—one of Walt Disney's first animators back in the 1930s.[2] Since Walt Disney himself preferred to think in terms of pictures rather than words, he embraced the use of storyboards for developing all his animated films. Similarly, when he created Disneyland in the 1950s, Walt Disney did not feel that floor plans and architectural renderings represented the sum total of a guest experience. So he brought storyboarding techniques from his film studio to the development of the attractions there.[3] This technique was seamlessly adopted, as Disneyland was essentially planned as a three-dimensional film and the early Imagineers were also studio animators. Today, Walt Disney Imagineers still use storyboards in planning Disney theme park attractions.

To create a storyboard, the Imagineers draw sketches and pin them to large wood-frame panels. Each sketch depicts a scene in a logical story sequence. Together, these reflect the beginning, middle, and end of the guest experience. Storyboard panels can include character poses, mood, color styling, scenery, and props. New ideas are pitched to the team, and scenes might be switched out after strengths and weaknesses are discussed and debated. The completed storyboard offers team members the first chance to experience a new attraction or show and see how the idea might—or might not—work.[4]

From Walt Disney's initial use of storyboards in his animated films, storyboards soon became widespread throughout the film industry. In more recent years, they have been applied to numerous other industries, including advertising, animation projects, comic books, videography, web development, software development, instructional design, and creative problem solving in school classrooms. Dozens of websites are devoted to explaining storyboarding techniques, including detailed instructions and templates geared to a variety of users.[5]

## Writing a Walkthrough

The visitor experience walkthrough becomes a tool for you to "storyboard" the experience of your historical environment without having to be an artist. Going through the process of imagining the visitor experience and writing this walkthrough

- ensures that the story and experience will have continuity;
- helps you see how your initial concept, historical research, and backstory translate into the physical space;
- allows you to envision the experience in ways that floor plans and lists alone cannot convey; and
- helps the whole team visualize the experience.

With this technique, it becomes obvious to see where you need to develop your experience in more detail and where you need to make it more active. If all visitors are doing in your walkthrough is looking and reading, maybe you need to think more creatively about the experience. The visitor experience walkthrough also has its obvious limits. In real life, different visitors would experience the space in different ways. Like the backstory, it serves primarily as a planning tool for you to envision the environment before committing to its actual layout and installation.

---

**CHECKLIST 6.1**
**Writing a Visitor Experience Walkthrough**

1. Select an imaginary visitor or visitor group from your target audience.
2. Putting yourself in their shoes, imagine walking through the experience.
3. Write out what they experience step by step, including visuals, multisensory, and interpretive elements. Note what impressions they are getting out of what they are experiencing.
4. Repeat with other visitor types or groups if desired.

---

## REAL-LIFE EXAMPLE: EXCERPT FROM THE VISITOR EXPERIENCE WALKTHROUGH FOR THE J. R. JONES GENERAL STORE[6]

The displays of products in each window draw our visitor's attention. On the left is a very appealing display of fishing rods and reels, decoys, and trout baskets, along with a pile of baseballs, baseball bats, and baseball players' caps. Next to this display is a handwritten sign that reads, "NEW SUPPLY OF SPORTING GOODS JUST IN." On the right is a rather jumbled pile of canned goods, to our visitor's eye somewhat different from the neat and conscious displays combining products and advertising in his local supermarket. Just before he enters the store, our visitor notices on his map that a special theatrical presentation will take place inside this store in fifteen minutes, so he decides to check out the place and wait for the presentation. He opens the door and steps inside.

The place seems dark at first. His senses are assaulted by pungent odors like polished wood, coffee, and tobacco. As he looks around, he is nearly overwhelmed by the visual richness of the objects—their color, their variety, the sheer quantity of goods. After a little closer scrutiny, he realizes that the products, which at first seemed a jumble, are in fact organized into groupings of similar things, and that there are large quantities of the same products, just as in stores he shops at himself.

## LAYOUT AND INSTALLATION

Once you are satisfied with the visitor experience of your environment from the written walkthrough, you can now translate the details of the walkthrough into a visual layout. If you are working with an exhibition designer, chances are that this has already begun—at least the dimensions of the overall space will have been determined and perhaps large artifacts will have been placed on a visual plan. The most important reason for going through this step is to be assured that everything will fit in the space—that a piece of furniture is going to fit within it, that you haven't spent unnecessary expense on more objects than you need, or, conversely, that you've planned enough objects so that the space does not look too sparse.

In planning the layout, it is helpful to imagine the people who might once have inhabited this space (or a space like this). How might they have made the space their own? How can you make it look as if these people have just left the room? Even though you always want to aim for historical accuracy, keep in mind that this environment also needs to tell a story in a three-dimensional way—a way that transforms all your rigorous research and creative thinking into a cohesive and emotionally compelling three-dimensional environment. As you imagine your layout, keep in mind Stephen Bitgood's six factors that create the feeling of immersion: realism of the illusion, dimensionality, multisensory stimulation, mental imagery, lack of interfering factors, and meaningfulness (see chapter 1 for a refresher).

Beyond three-dimensional storytelling, the layout should also address such logistics and operational requirements as

- how lighting, sound, and tactile elements will work;
- how interactives will be integrated;
- how natural and designed barriers will fit the space;
- additional seating that might be needed for visitor comfort;
- visitor flow;
- staffing needs;
- accessibility concerns;
- cleaning and maintenance requirements;
- visitor and staff safety (such as uneven floors, low lights, and low ceilings);
- care of collections (such as the need for low light levels, environmental controls, and window treatments); and

- artifact security issues (including potential theft as well as damage by weather, vibration, and falls).[7]

As a result of assessing these, such controls as alarms and locks, barriers, safety wire, security systems, and smoke alarms might be needed. Also keep in mind that any of these decisions might have to be adjusted later as you observe the space when it opens to the public.

Today, various computer software programs can help you experiment with visual layouts.[8] You can also physically arrange paper cutouts of objects drawn to scale on a measured floor plan of the space. Simply sketching out object placements and other components on a floor plan also helps, or you can experiment with arranging actual objects on pieces of drawn-to-scale butcher paper and photographing your preferred arrangements (see Figure 6.1).

When you are satisfied with the plan for your layout—and as long as the physical space is ready, objects and reproductions have been obtained, and the interpretive techniques you planned have been produced or fabricated—

**Figure 6.1. Before final reproductions and artifacts were determined, potential items for each shelf of the J. R. Jones Store were arranged on drawn-to-scale pieces of butcher paper. This pre-installation step also led to such design solutions as installing pegs to display kerosene lamp chimneys.**
Photo by Deborah Berk

the time of installation is finally at hand! If you have planned well and thought out as many of the details as possible, it should be an enjoyable and satisfying experience.

## REAL-LIFE EXAMPLE: 1973 "BACK-TO-THE-LAND" COMMUNE, *YOUR PLACE IN TIME* EXHIBITION

The initial plan for this space was that it would be open and completely accessible to visitors. But as planning ensued, it seemed that a look-in would help make the story and message tighter and easier to convey. The triangular elements created by the steel structure of the geodesic dome structure afforded a natural barrier, supplemented by pieces of Plexiglas placed within the triangles at the lower levels. While not as interactive as originally planned, we do believe that this has kept the environment intact in a way that has actually encouraged more successful immersion than if visitors entered and walked around the space.

Using the designer's measured drawing of the space, we sketched out many layout ideas, inspired by images from the *Shelter* publication and making sure we had scaled measurements of the larger artifacts. In the limited space, we came up with a plan for a half living room–type space and half cooking-and-eating space, with the two separated by the coal-burning stove in the center. Many times, we arranged smaller groupings of objects that we had obtained on measured pieces of butcher paper to see how they might fit and how they might look on, say, the bookshelves, the kitchen table, the top of the cabinet, and the top of the refrigerator and then photographed our favored arrangements (see Figure 1.4).

At the time of installation, we also implemented one last addition to enhance realism and the presence of people. Inspired by an in-process whist game that is displayed on a table in the lobby of the Hollywood Tower Hotel at Walt Disney World's Hollywood Studios, we asked staff members to "play" an ongoing game of chess on the chess board that was displayed in the living room–type space. In this way, when the installation was completed, the in-process chess game would look authentic, while it would also seem as if the people who were playing the game had just left the room (as seen in Figure 6.3, the look of this "in-process" game has been difficult to maintain over time). Finally, we felt that posting a handwritten "job list" on the refrigerator, looking as if commune members had created it for the day, would clearly reinforce the idea of people living together in this communal space.

Figure 6.2. Object groupings for the commune environment—like the table setting, refrigerator and cabinet tops, and cabinet shelves—were arranged in different configurations, then photographed in preparation for final installation.

Photo by Deborah Berk

## INTERPRETIVE TRAINING

Whether interpreters are expected to be stationed in a historic structure, to staff a historical vignette, or to give walking tours, you will want to communicate your vision to them through a formal training session.[9] It is important to remember that these should involve not only *what* interpreters say but also *how* they say it. Time should be planned into the formal training for interpreters to practice before they are stationed on-site—to absorb all the information that has been given to them about content, audience, and delivery; to structure their presentation; and to shape their unique interpretive style. This should involve practicing on their own, shadowing experienced presenters, and getting positive and useful feedback from peers and supervisors.

### Written Interpretive Manual

As part of their training, interpreters should be provided with a written interpretive manual that they can reference in an ongoing way. In my Technical Leaflet, "Not Just a Bunch of Facts: Creating Dynamic Interpretive Manuals," I argue that written manuals for interpretive staff should not be simply a fragmented collection of information but a hierarchically organized grouping of materials that, at all times, aims to facilitate effective interpretation.[10] Written interpretive manuals can also help to

- provide consistency for staff at all levels of the institution about the goals and themes of the project;
- document the rigorous and creative work that went into the planning of the project;
- provide updated information for interpretive staff with the assurance that the new information will continue to hone to the original vision; and
- provide a concrete tool for training, program assessment, and staff evaluation.

The following is a recommended organizational plan for a written interpretive manual based upon the approach of a hierarchical structure of information.

Following the table of contents, the front section contains the most important information for interpreters to know and provides the framework for everything that follows in the rest of the manual. These elements should be written in a bullet-point or brief narrative format so they are easy to read and can be referenced at a glance:

- Big Idea/Main Message and Interpretive Themes—as described in chapter 3

- Mission Connection—how your environment relates to and supports your museum's mission
- Relevant Connections between Past and Present—how your historical themes and topics are relevant to people's lives today
- Visitor Outcomes—as described in chapter 3
- Sample Story—Writing the main ideas in the form of a story establishes a narrative format from the beginning, reinforcing the idea that this manual—and effective interpretation in general—is not just a collection of facts.
- Key Presentation Points—a list of key points for interpreters to consider in creating their own versions of the story
- List of Interpretive Techniques and Program Elements

The rest of the manual should build upon the information in the front section, organized in a way that is keyed back to these elements, easy to locate, and written in a straightforward and readable manner. This information should include

- additional historical background;
- audience engagement strategies;
- presentation delivery techniques; and
- general logistics.

Because ongoing revisions to the written manual are inevitable, it is best to maintain an easy-to-locate electronic version of it in order to quickly make changes and disseminate new information as it becomes available as well as to be able to distribute an updated version of the entire manual annually.

## IMMEDIATE ADJUSTMENTS

Sometimes, after opening to the public, it becomes apparent rather quickly that something you planned is just not working. You might notice this yourself or get feedback from interpreters. Your Big Idea/Main Message or interpretive themes may be too complex for interpreters to convey or for visitors to grasp. Your interpretive techniques don't seem to work the way you had envisioned, as visitors seem confused by them, don't do what you had intended them to, or just plain ignore them. Sometimes, no amount of prototyping (let alone no prototyping at all!) can help you know exactly what will happen when your environment is complete and open to the public. You must be open to revision and refinement. Ideally, this can be done before the momentum of completing the project fades, the budget disappears, and people move on to other things.

## POST-OPENING EVALUATION

Formalized evaluation can be undertaken at or soon after project completion. This can include the types of evaluation generally referred to as remedial and summative. With time, budget, resources, and momentum, these types of evaluation can allow for modification of components (e.g., placement and content of labels) or simply provide valuable findings for future projects.

Remedial evaluation encourages fine-tuning with newly completed projects or the refinement and renewal of older projects.[11] It is useful for addressing problems that could not be foreseen during the project's development. For example, are there problems that appear after installation with lighting, traffic flow, wayfinding, or placement of labels? Through formalized observations and/or interviews, this type of evaluation can provide a check that the environment "works" in a practical sense, determine ongoing maintenance or other resource issues, provide early insights into what visitors are getting out of the experience, and improve its short- or longer-term effectiveness for visitors.

Summative evaluation assesses the effectiveness of the project as it relates to the initial goals laid out at its onset.[12] Do the final product and its individual components align with what was intended? Typical questions that might be incorporated into a summative evaluation include the following:

- What meaning (in the broadest sense) has the visitor created from his/ her experience?
- What is most compelling?
- What is most surprising?
- What is confusing/not understandable?
- Do visitors read the labels? Which ones? For how long?
- Are visitors operating the interactives properly?
- Which components attract the most/least attention?
- How much time do visitors spend there?[13]

Summative evaluation typically involves a fairly large sample size and a variety of evaluation instruments and it usually requires formal evaluation training or outside experts. The most common evaluation instrument is a questionnaire that asks open-ended, qualitative questions and discerns overall patterns of visitor understanding and learning, determining what components or aspects are most compelling and what is confusing. Quantitative measures of satisfaction can also be included. Complementing these, summative evaluation also often includes a timing and tracking study—a quantitative, numerically based and statistically analyzed study of where visitors stopped and in what order, how long they spent reading labels and doing interactives, and overall time in the space. These interviews often reveal surprises, reflecting the complexity and diversity of human behavior.

## MAINTAINING THE ENVIRONMENT

You may think that when you have installed your environment, trained inter-preters, provided them with a written manual, and even made some adjust-ments to the installation, you are finished. But you are never really finished. Things fade. Things break. Things mysteriously "walk off." Your attempt to purposefully "mess up" a space to make it look lived in might inadvertently get "tidied up" by well-meaning cleaning staff (see Figure 6.3). Because of these likely possibilities, it is crucial to communicate your intent to all staff members who will be coming in contact with this installation and to plan ahead for replacements.

**Figure 6.3.  Object groupings that are purposely intended to show a "lived-in" quality are particularly difficult to maintain over time, like the business papers scattered across J. R. Jones' desk.**
Photo by Deborah Berk

It takes a continual effort to make sure that the environment you worked so hard to create continues to look as "spot on" as when you first completed it. This starts with a formalized maintenance plan—that is, a plan for who will maintain the environment to keep it working, looking the same, and making sure it is viable for visitors.[14] Money should be built into your museum operations budget to cover costs associated with its upkeep.

Written documentation is a crucial part of a continuing maintenance plan.[15] A "maintenance bible" is important to retain cohesion for those who need to fix, rework, or replace elements of the experience. This will help them to know how these elements were originally made, what materials and specifications were used, and from what sources they were obtained. The documentation should be accurate and accessible, clearly organized, and stored in a convenient form, whether physical or electronic. Completed as the project is wrapping up, this can include as-built drawings; paint specifications; a final collections list; photographic rights documentation; the maintenance manual; final costs (including staff time, if possible); schedules for replacing lighting fixtures; sources and warranties for replacement parts; specs on barriers; audio, video, and dramatic performance scripts; label proofs; music playlists; and, if revisions are determined, a plan for implementing these.

For curators, conservators, and collections managers, it is important to take—and keep in an accessible place—record photographs; a detailed inventory of the final environment; a list of all the sources for reproductions (and costs); and a collections rotation schedule, including dates that loans need to be returned. The environment should be reviewed against the photographs and inventory at least annually—with revisions, refinements, and replacements noted and a plan made to implement any changes.

## ONGOING REFINEMENTS

While a maintenance plan helps you retain the consistency of your environment so that everything looks exactly the same as the day it opened, you should also be open to refinements that enhance and improve the visitor experience over time. This might be due to changing institutional priorities, evolving programs, and newly targeted audiences. As McKenna-Cress and Kamien remark in their book *Creating Exhibitions: Collaboration in the Planning, Development, and Design of Innovative Experiences*, "continuous nurturing" helps you "keep up with contemporary audiences in an ever-changing society."[16]

How can you "nurture" your historical environment to ensure that it has continuing relevance and impact? Here are some strategies to consider, based upon real-life examples:

1. Incorporate elements into your environment that align with new program and special event offerings.

A few years after the unstaffed McGuffey Birthplace was open to the public, an institutional decision was made to staff the building during its new Fall Flavors Weekends in September and October and its Holiday Nights program in December. During these times, third-person interpreters, wearing historic clothing of the 1800–1802 era, demonstrate cooking techniques and food practices of the McGuffey family while also incorporating the building's Main Message and interpretive themes into their presentation. As visitors see smoke rising from the chimney, hear the crackling fireplace, and smell the redolent odors of food cooking over the open fireplace, the multisensory experience becomes a powerful draw and entrée to the story (see Figure 6.4). During these programs, the plexiglas is removed from the cupboard shelves.

**Figure 6.4. Fireplace cooking at McGuffey Birthplace during Fall Flavors Weekends in Greenfield Village.**
Photo by Caroline Braden

2. Adapt planned and existing interpretive techniques to new audiences.

An early, overly ambitious plan for the daily program at the J. R. Jones General Store—to have interpreters move from shelf to shelf around the store, picking up objects and "filling out" orders related to actual 1880s-era customers—was abandoned fairly quickly when the reinstalled building first opened. But it has successfully re-emerged as customized offerings for special targeted audiences. The customer orders idea works particularly well with small groups, like educators attending training programs and K–12 audiences in which breakout groups are given the role of specific customers and the assignment to create a shopping list for their customer (with the aid of interpreters). The objects that were designated for handling in putting together these customer orders are now being used to develop tactile tours for people who are blind or visually impaired, along with the addition of new sensory opportunities like smelling spices and tea, which has also enhanced the experience for all visitors (see Figure 6.5). Because of its great potential for sparking memories, this

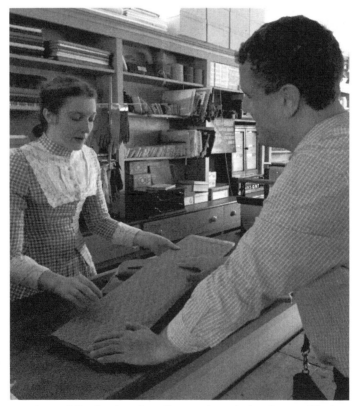

**Figure 6.5.   A specially developed tactile tour for people who are blind or visually impaired is in progress at the J. R. Jones General Store.**
Photo by Caroline Braden

environment also lends itself to special programs for people who have early stages of dementia and their care partners.

3. Be attuned to ways in which your environment's relevance can change over time.

The "Back-to-the-Land" Commune in the *Your Place in Time* exhibition is now taking on new relevance and context—particularly with contemporary interest in such trends as organic farming and foods, vegetarianism, DIY crafts, and sustainable energy sources—all foundational during this era and visible in this environment.[17] Based upon a recent visitor study, younger audiences who have no personal memories of this era are finding it meaningful in their own ways. This is an example of how, over time, changing audiences and trends can alter attitudes toward, and make new meaning of, a historical environment.

## WRAPPING IT UP

Over the last four chapters, I have described the process of creating historical environments step by step—from framing your project to determining your research methodology to creating a backstory, interpretive strategy, and furnishings plan, to—finally—installing, adjusting, evaluating, and refining the actual three-dimensional environment. You now possess the tools to create your own environments that are institutionally aligned, historically accurate, and engaging to visitors.

The case studies I described in these chapters were intended to serve as teaching tools so you could clearly see how each part of the process has its place in the bigger picture, and how they all work together. But these are just a few examples. There are numerous other historical environments that both reinforce the process I have described and offer new insights into the ways in which these environments can be envisioned. The next chapter describes several examples.

## NOTES

1. Walkthroughs are described in Kathleen McLean, *Planning for People in Museum Exhibitions* (Washington, DC: The Association of Science-Technology Centers, 1993), 12; Polly McKenna-Cress and Janet Kamien, *Creating Exhibitions: Collaboration in the Planning, Development, and Design of Innovative Experiences* (Hoboken, NJ: John Wiley and Sons, 2013), 231; and Marianna Curling, "How to Write a Furnishing Plan," *History News* 57, no. 2 (Spring 2002): Technical Leaflet #218, 3.

2. Disney Institute, *Be Our Guest: Perfecting the Art of Customer Service* (New York: Disney Editions, 2001), 191.

3. Disney Institute, *Be Our Guest*, 192.

4. The Imagineers, *Walt Disney Imagineering*, 40–41; Disney Institute, *Be Our Guest*, 192.

5. See, for example, Aaron Sherman, "What Is a Storyboard?" Storyboard That website (blog), accessed March 21, 2018, http://www.storyboardthat.com/blog/e/what-is-a-storyboard; and Caroline Mercurio, "The Benefits of Storyboards and How to Use Them," Storyblocks Videoblocks website, August 24, 2011, accessed April 29, 2018, https://content.videoblocks.com/video-basics/the-benefits-of-storyboards-and-how-to-use-them/. See also "Part 6. Pitching and Feedback," Pixar in a Box website, accessed July 14, 2018, https://www.khanacademy.org/partner-content/pixar/storytelling/storyboard-your-film/v/pitching-feedback and https://www.khanacademy.org/partner-content/pixar/storytelling/storyboard-your-film/v/pitching1.

6. "The J. R. Jones General Store in Greenfield Village, Program Plan," Donna R. Braden and Blake D. Hayes (unpublished manuscript, 15 September 1992), Braden Papers.

7. For more detail on operational issues to consider, see Bradley Brooks, "The Historic House Furnishings Plan: Process and Product," in *Interpreting Historic House Museums*, ed. Jessica Foy Donnelly (Walnut Creek, CA: AltaMira Press, a Division of Rowman & Littlefield, 2002), 139–41; and Mick Woodcock, "Physical Control for Collections: Keeping It on the Table after Bringing It All to the Table," *Proceedings of the 2013 Conference and Annual Meeting, Hale Farm & Village, Akron, Ohio*, ed. Debra A. Reid, vol. XXXVI (North Bloomfield, OH: The Association for Living History, Farm and Agricultural Museums, 2014): 105–107.

8. SketchUp is a commonly used software for constructing digital models of exhibitions. Mentions of this software can be found in John Summers, *Creating Exhibits That Engage: A Manual for Museums and Historical Organizations* (Lanham, MD: Rowman & Littlefield/AASLH, 2018), 110; and Alice Parman, Ann Craig, Lyle Murphy, Liz White, and Lauren Willis, *Exhibit Makeovers: A Do-It Yourself Workbook for Small Museums*, 2nd ed. (Lanham, MD: Rowman & Littlefield/AASLH, 2017), 65. A variety of easy-to-use interior decorating and space planning software, aimed at people arranging furnishings in their homes, can also be used for simple exhibit and room layouts. See, for example, a description of Floorplanner in Nina Simon's "Quick Hit: A Free Tech Tool for Exhibit Layout," Museum 2.0 website (blog), September 15, 2010, accessed May 14, 2018, http://museumtwo.blogspot.com/2010/09/quick-hit-free-tech-tool-for-exhibit.html; and Ronique Gibson's "10 Best Online Virtual Room Programs and Tools," Freshome website, July 5, 2015, accessed May 14, 2018, https://freshome.com/10-best-free-online-virtual-room-programs-and-tools/.

9. Much has been written about interpretive training sessions and components. See, for example, the numerous insightful essays in *Interpreting Historic House Museums*, ed. Jessica Foy Donnelly (Lanham, MD: AltaMira Press, a Division of Rowman & Littlefield, 2002); Stephen Hague, "How to Plan and Implement Interpretation," *History News* 68, no. 2 (Spring 2013): Technical Leaflet #262; Barbara Abramoff Levy, Sandra McKenzie Lloyd, and Susan Porter Schreiber, *Great Tours! Thematic Tours and Guide Training for Historic Sites* (Walnut Creek, CA: AltaMira Press, a Division of Rowman & Littlefield, 2001); Stacy F. Roth, *Past into Present: Effec-*

*tive Techniques for First-Person Historical Interpretation* (Chapel Hill: University of North Carolina Press, 1998); and Michael P. Gross and Ron Zimmerman, "Park and Museum Interpretation: Helping Visitors Find Meaning," *Curator: The Museum Journal* 45, no. 4 (October 2002): 265–76. The table on page 274 was created as part of the National Park Service's Interpretive Development Program. See this Program's current "Foundational Competencies for All Interpreters," National Park Service US Department of the Interior Interpretive Development Program website. Accessed July 15, 2018, https://www.nps.gov/idp/interp/101/module.htm.

10. Donna R. Braden, "Not Just a Bunch of Facts: Crafting Dynamic Interpretive Manuals," *History News* 69, no. 3 (Summer 2014): Technical Leaflet #267.

11. Helpful published works on remedial evaluation include Mark Walhimer, "Museum Exhibition Design, Part VI. Exhibition Evaluation," Museum Planner website (blog), July 10, 2012, accessed July 9, 2018, https://museumplanner.org/museum-exhibition-design-part-vi/; McKenna-Cress and Kamien, *Creating Exhibitions*, 293–94; and Beverly Serrell, *Exhibit Labels: An Interpretive Approach*, 2nd ed. (Lanham, MD: Rowman & Littlefield, 2015), 302–303.

12. Recommended published works on summative evaluation include *Introduction to Museum Evaluation*; Stein, Adams, and Luke, "Thinking Evaluatively"; McKenna-Cress and Kamien, *Creating Exhibitions*, 295; Serrell, *Exhibit Labels*, 302–24; and McLean, *Planning for People in Museum Exhibitions*, 75–80.

13. Randi Korn, "Studying Your Visitors: Where to Begin," in *Introduction to Museum Evaluation*, 8.

14. For more on maintenance plans, see McKenna-Cress and Kamien, *Creating Exhibitions*, 296.

15. For more on project documentation, see McKenna-Cress and Kamien, *Creating Exhibitions*, 298–99.

16. McKenna-Cress and Kamien, *Creating Exhibitions*, 296.

17. One example that is indicative of the current interest in these topics is Jonathan Kauffman's book, *Hippie Food: How Back-to-the-Landers, Longhairs, and Revolutionaries Changed the Way We Eat* (New York: HarperCollins, 2018).

# A Sampling of Historical Environments

Today, numerous imaginative, engaging, and effective historical environments can be found in museums large and small, indoor and outdoor, with sizable budgets and miniscule ones. The examples described in this chapter suggest the range and variety of these environments at museums of varying size and scope. Each example offers strategies, ideas, and lessons learned that can help you as you plan or re-envision your own historical environments. Feel free to pick and choose ideas from any of these. My aim here is to show how—through purposeful intent, a planned methodology, visitor focus, and staff creativity—engaging and memorable historical environments can be created at virtually any institution.

As you read this, you may find that some of these examples were developed a while back. Of course there are numerous others that I could have selected. However, I felt that these case studies, drawn from both museum exhibitions and historic sites, presented a wide range of exemplars that address key elements laid out in this book, including sound methodology, successful immersion, visitor engagement, and ongoing refinement.

## TWO BENCHMARK EXAMPLES

The first two examples described here—the Tenement Museum on Manhattan's Lower East Side and the *Open House: If These Walls Could Talk* exhibition at Minnesota History Center in St. Paul—have been written about so often I debated even including them. But, in the end, I felt that I would be remiss if I left them out of this chapter. Both the Tenement Museum's furnished spaces in two historic structures and the *Open House* exhibition not only embody the key points I address in this book; they both forge new ground—breaking out of the mold of traditional interpretive strategies and furnishings plans.

## The Tenement Museum, New York, New York[1]

The Tenement Museum has been called "one of the most innovative and compelling interpretive sites of immigrant and urban history in the United States."[2] Through recreated apartments and businesses of real families in two historic tenement buildings, the Museum tells the stories of immigrants who started their lives anew on Manhattan's Lower East Side between the nineteenth and twenty-first centuries. Making the best use of the buildings' small spaces, visitors take guided tours through the apartments in small groups, allowing a conversational experience. Engaging, enthusiastic, and extremely knowledgeable educators (using the Tenement Museum's parlance) give these tours, focusing upon personalized family stories, broader context related to these stories, and insights into current debates about immigration and public health.

Visitors feel utterly transported through time when they enter restored tenement apartments that have been recreated through painstaking historical research. An abundant use of reproduction and representative objects (rather than solely unique collection items) means that no stanchions or barriers are required, so visitors can easily imagine family members inhabiting the spaces. Apartments are lit using period fixtures and natural lighting and presented as if the inhabitants' daily lives were interrupted at that precise moment in time, for example, a garment worker's basket with piecework in progress or a meal in the midst of being prepared.

In 2012, the Museum expanded its offerings at 97 Orchard Street with a "Shop Life" tour, tracing the stories of several businesses that operated in this building. This tour marked several new directions for the museum. The tour starts with the story of the German family who once operated the first-floor saloon, but it goes on to cover more than 100 years of the building's history, during which several store owners ran businesses here. An unrestored area includes a case display of related commercial objects found in the building. This was also the Tenement Museum's first tour to extend into the building's basement, where interactive multimedia (also tried for the first time) augments the personal stories told by the educators. This interpretive tool encourages visitors to select historic objects and use an embedded RFID code to discover for themselves the stories of businesses that operated here.

Since its beginning, the Tenement Museum has given prime importance to visitor accessibility, welcoming people of all backgrounds and abilities. Each educator works with individuals and groups to provide the best possible experience, while additional tools like assistive listening devices, visitor seating, touchable objects, and large-print and Braille versions of handouts are available during the tours. "Shop Life" was also the first tour at the Tenement Museum to be wheelchair accessible.

In 2017, the Tenement Museum opened its "Under One Roof" tour. Here, visitors walk through one apartment at 103 Orchard Street that represents the homes of three post–World War II families who settled here—Jewish Holocaust survivors, Puerto Rican migrants, and Chinese immigrants. This tour is recent enough in time that the families themselves have provided memories and photographs to add authenticity to the furnishings and interpretation. "Under One Roof," accessible by elevator, also includes a recreated Chinatown garment factory with stories told through interactive multimedia integrated with touchable artifacts in the space.

Visitor evaluation of these tours has shown a long-lasting impact and a high degree of follow-up actions, such as asking a relative about family history or checking out a library book about a topic discovered on the tour. Michelle Moon, chief programs officer at the Tenement Museum, remarks that:

> Visitors tend to retain strong sense memories from their Tenement Museum experience, finding the spaces, lighting, displays, and stories deeply evocative. The immersion comes not only from the physical surrounding, but from the practice of "facilitated storytelling" that invites them to connect the family stories they hear on the tours with their own experiences—whether a family history of immigration or just the experience of being a newcomer, enduring hardship, or working hard to get ahead. The combination of space and story adds up to a powerful history experience.

## OPEN HOUSE: IF THESE WALLS COULD TALK EXHIBITION, MINNESOTA HISTORY CENTER, ST. PAUL, MINNESOTA[3]

This exhibition, which opened in 2006, defined a new approach to storytelling in an exhibition gallery while, at the same time, paying obsessive attention to real stories from a real house. *Open House* focuses on a single, ordinary house in St. Paul's gritty East Side and the people who made that house their home from 1888 to the present—from the first German immigrants through the Italians, African Americans, and Hmong who succeeded them. A recreated house (the actual house is still in its original location), fifty families, and 118 years of habitation are presented in a 5,200-square-foot exhibition.

Benjamin Filene, who was the senior exhibit developer for *Open House*, has related that the exhibition team set out "to capture history's inherent messiness—to tell a story that was not a straight line with ready-made lessons, to let the lives of real people from the past guide us in directions that we had not mapped out in advance."[4] To accomplish this, they not only did extensive primary source research but also met with the people who had lived and were still living in the house as well as engaging community groups to share in the spirit of discovery and reflection.

When visitors enter the "house" and walk through the "rooms," they feel as if they have been transported to another time. They "meet" the residents through a series of furnished rooms arranged in a sequence over time, each revealing stories about a different family or cluster of families. By exploring each room and interacting with the items in it, visitors actively explore and discover clues to each of these stories.

To attain this level of interactivity, the exhibit team rethought virtually everything about traditionally furnished and interpreted spaces. First, they dispensed with the traditional notion of the period room. The spaces are fully realized three-dimensional settings but without barriers. People take center stage in each space, with the help of clues provided by props, replica furnishings, indestructible artifacts, and the rooms' structural and decorative details.

Next, the team rethought the notion of traditional label text—except at entry "doorways" that describe the inhabitants of each new era and on "windows" in each room that present broader context (with text cleverly titled "A Look Outside"). Instead of traditional labels, words appear or pop up only within the context of the story—for example, on the floor, on a chenille bedspread, inside a lunchbox, or on a series of recreated lantern slides. Finally, although interactive media are embedded throughout the exhibit, it is virtually invisible to visitors. Instead, it becomes apparent only when visitors touch or manipulate objects. While visitors can interact with everything and the rooms provide a sort of theatrical backdrop to this interactivity, every story comes from a specific, real person. Nothing is made up.

This exhibition has a powerful impact on visitors, particularly in terms of personal meaning-making. Not only do they learn something about the past residents of this house but they also tend to use the exhibition as a setting in which to reflect upon their own personal pasts. Summative evaluation findings have suggested that visitors move here at a slower pace than the other exhibitions in the Museum, that they linger longer (there are forty-two contextual places on which visitors can sit in the exhibition!), and that at least some of them are likely to carry home a new or renewed interest in tracing the history of their own family or house. As Filene has recounted, "*Open House* started as an effort to give voice to forgotten people in history; in the end, it allowed visitors to recognize that they themselves have something to say."[5]

The following examples include historical environments from several other museum exhibitions and historic structures. In each of these, the environments play a key role, often a transformative one for the museums, their staff, their communities, and their visitors.

## HISTORICAL ENVIRONMENTS IN MUSEUM EXHIBITIONS

### The *1950s: Building the American Dream* Exhibition, The Ohio History Connection, Columbus, Ohio[6]

After acquiring a 1949 prefabricated Lustron House, the staff at the Ohio History Connection decided to use it to create a completely hands-on experience—an experience that would be engaging, interesting, and even a little fun in addition to addressing clearly articulated learning goals.

#### Planning

The Ohio History Connection, formerly the Ohio Historical Society, is a statewide history organization with its mission to spark discovery of Ohio's stories by encouraging people to embrace the present, share the past, and transform the future. The *1950s: Building the American Dream* exhibition, which opened in July 2013, was created to align with its strategic goal of encouraging visitors to experience Ohio history more actively and from a more personal viewpoint. This experience offers an immersion into life in the 1950s as seen through the eyes of one Ohio family, with a visit to the family's fully furnished ranch-style home—an all-steel Lustron House prefabricated in a Columbus factory after World War II.

Front-end evaluation led the Museum to focus on the broader message of life during the 1950s rather than a specific emphasis on the manufacture of the Lustron House. Testing also informed the direction of a participatory approach, as respondents showed an interest in activities such as games, music, and "attempting cooking."

The primary target audience for the exhibition was intergenerational families.

#### Research

Historical research involved consulting numerous secondary sources about daily life and the growth of suburbia in the 1950s, as well as delving into primary sources related to home furnishings, design, and the Lustron Corporation. Primary sources included the 1953 Montgomery Ward & Company catalog; popular magazines such as *McCall's* and *Better Homes and Gardens*; the home furnishings book, *How to Decorate and Light your*

*Home*, by E. W. Commery and Eugene Stephenson; the book *Guide to Easier Living* by industrial designer Russel Wright and his wife, Mary; business and design records from the Lustron Manufacturing Corporation; and oral histories with staff who had worked for the company.

### Furnishings and Interpretation

The planning team created backstories, or general character sketches, for the four main family members who would be "inhabiting" this house. Using the research and these backstories as a guide, curators created ideal object lists for each room with the understanding that all objects needed to be touchable. Reproductions were used when originals were not available or when team members felt the originals were too delicate. A few nontouchable collections items were placed behind Plexiglas, although the staff worked hard to minimize this.

Visitors walking through the home can see and feel what it was like to live in that era (see Figure 7.1). Smells of fresh-cut grass, laundry, and cookies

**Figure 7.1.    A visitor peruses towels, linens, and bedspreads in a closet of the Lustron House.**
Courtesy of the Ohio History Connection

waft through the air. Sounds are present outside and in the house. Radio and television broadcasts can be heard and watched. After their walkthrough of the house, visitors can learn more about the 1950s through videos with recollections of Ohioans who grew up in the era, plus displays that feature TV, radio, movies, books, and other popular culture of the time.

Furnishings, lighting, smells, and sounds in the house are changed out through the holiday season (Halloween through New Year's). Interpretive floor staff occasionally play the role of 1950s-era characters (family members as well as peripheral characters such as a mailman, repairman, and neighbor) in the space, but they are trained to give visitors time and space to linger on their own. Members of the interpretive staff occasionally create their own special tours or programs in the house. During the busy school group season, staff members are added at the front and back doors to help handle crowds.

## Maintenance and Refinement

Because of the hands-on, interactive nature of this experience, much attention has been paid to ongoing upkeep. Interpretive floor staff and housekeeping staff are constantly suggesting adjustments to make the house both a better environment for visitors and one that is easier to maintain. Weekly cleaning of the house is required and a range of items has been replaced. The Museum has experienced little if any theft from the items that are accessible to the visitors but some have been broken and have needed to be replaced. Some of the highly interactive elements have had to be removed, such as an operating record player (which broke easily) and the fake food (which kept breaking and was very expensive). But, generally, the main components of the experience have remained intact.

## Relevance and Impact

A summative evaluation of this experience has revealed that visitors find it informative, personally meaningful, emotionally compelling, and memorable. It is often cited as their favorite part of visiting the Museum. According to Megan Wood, director of Museum and Library Services, the most memorable aspect of this experience is visitors' ability to "free-play in the space" as well as to talk not only within their own social group but also with visitors they don't even know. As far as its relevance to visitors, Wood feels that:

Almost everyone, no matter their background, recognizes something in the house. Adults visiting with children explain things like the rotary dial phone, the toys, and the kitchen wares and talk about family members who are gone. The time period is both close and distant and the experience literally brings it to life.

## Recreated Barracks Spaces, Heart Mountain Interpretive Center, near Cody, Wyoming[7]

In 2012, the exhibition in this interpretive learning center, *Across the Wire: Voices from Heart Mountain*, received an Excellence in Exhibition award from the American Alliance of Museums for its "sensitive and eloquent presentation of a difficult topic."[8] The creative conceptualization and design of two immersive barracks spaces in this exhibition provide a visceral and emotionally powerful way for visitors to imagine what it was like for Japanese and Japanese American internees to be confined here during World War II.

### Planning

The Heart Mountain Interpretive Center opened in August 2011, dedicated to passing on the Heart Mountain story to future generations. The Heart Mountain Wyoming Foundation defined the direction of the new visitor center, built on the site of the former Heart Mountain Relocation Center. The Foundation contracted with Split Rock Studios of St. Paul, Minnesota, to design and build the exhibition. An introductory film, produced by Oscar-winning filmmaker Steven Okazaki and Farallon Films, reinforced the exhibition storyline.

The primary goal of the entire exhibition was to express the idea that the forced relocation and confinement of Japanese Americans was unambiguously wrong. The injustice of the entire internment camp program, and specifically that at Heart Mountain, would be communicated through the singular voices of the actual people who had been imprisoned here. Sarah Bartlett, who was the Split Rock Studios exhibit developer for the project, recalled that using the "we" voice instead of "they" changed the whole tone of the exhibition. Not only did the "we" voice fit well with the goal of the Foundation to express *their* story from *their* point of view, but it immersed visitors by inviting them more directly into the story.

The idea of creating immersive spaces within the exhibition emerged fairly early in the project planning. Since the main experience of the Heart Mountain internees was one of being removed from familiar surroundings and their stable home life and placed in what was in essence a prison camp setting far from home, creating immersive spaces that embodied these ideas seemed crucial.

### Research

The historical research for these immersive spaces came from secondary sources as well as personal accounts, diaries, and camp newspapers of the time; government documents (carefully scrutinized for propaganda); memoirs written later, and oral histories. Numerous detailed photographs of buildings and their interiors taken by internees also served as invaluable resources. As Bartlett remarks:

> Immersive displays always involve a certain artificiality and theatricality, but basing the barracks on real references and getting regular input and criticism from people who actually experienced the barracks kept the exhibit from feeling fake or glib.

### Furnishings and Interpretation

The two immersive barracks rooms are seamlessly interwoven into a cohesive, chronological storyline within the exhibition—from developments during World War II leading to anti-Japanese resentment, to the ultimate decision to uproot Japanese and Japanese American people from their homes and remove them to faraway camps. These topics are communicated through historic photographs, scenic environments, environmental graphics, and first-person audio accounts that all enhance the "you are there" quality.

These two barracks rooms do not duplicate any specific one in a photograph but are generic recreations from several photographs. According to Christopher Wilson, Split Rock Studios senior designer, the first room is a small, empty space, intended to show "the shock value of a family's initial arrival at what was essentially a tarpaper shack, with no facilities, in a desert environment that was vastly different than the relatively lush environment in California" whence the families had come. A life-size cutout of a group of family members with their luggage (direct printed on Sintra, an expanded PVC, with a steel frame holding it up) appears in the center of the room, taken directly from a photograph of the era. It seems to fill the space, leaving one to wonder how these people actually fit anything else in it. The looks on family members' faces and the obvious dearth of belongings heighten the emotion of the scene. An audio conversation between family members conveys the overall shock and varying reactions of family members to coming here—from anger among the children to stoicism by the parents.

The second room is furnished to represent a later time, to show how these families used scavenged items and arranged their spaces to feel as much like "home" as they could manage (see Figure 1.2). The furnishings of this room came from a combination of places: items from internees and their descendants (artifacts and even suitcases still filled with belongings that had been stashed away by parents emerged out of sheds and closets during the exhibition development process); original pieces of Heart Mountain Relocation Center furniture made of scrap lumber found in an old barracks that had been moved after the war to Powell, Wyoming; and thrift shop items that matched the photographs. Bartlett recalls that:

The team insisted that the space had to look and feel real and not sanitized. Former internees had seen recreated barracks in other museums that looked too "nice" and had been stung by offhand remarks by general visitors to those exhibits that the experience of camp didn't look so bad. We sought out candid photographs of spaces that showed the realities of life in camp and did our best to replicate those conditions: water stains on the walls and ceiling, smoke from the stove, dust seeping in through cracks in the walls and windows, a chamber pot in one corner.

In this second room, some nonoriginal items were placed on the public side of the glass-wall barrier, as the Foundation wanted visitors to feel that they had truly "entered" these spaces at the same time that the original artifacts could be protected. The glass-wall barrier was chosen instead of a rail-type barrier not only for security reasons but, with few staff members on site, so that the artifacts would require less cleaning and maintenance over time (see Figure 7.2).

## Relevance and Impact

Visitor feedback to these immersive spaces has been very positive. Wilson admits that, while he has been designing exhibits for thirty-eight years, this is

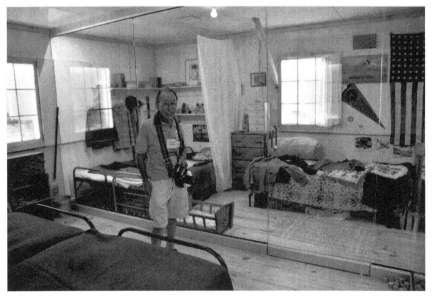

**Figure 7.2.** Cots and other furnishings of the internment camp barracks environment at Heart Mountain Interpretive Center, near Cody, Wyoming, continue on the other side of the glass wall barrier into the visitor space. Viewing this space is Mr. Bacon Sakatani, who was instrumental in the creation of this powerful interpretive center.
Courtesy of Christopher K. Wilson

one of his favorites. "These . . . stories grab you by the heart," Wilson admits. "The example is useful in people's lives. People need to know about it; it is so important." Bartlett adds that,

> Emotion is such an important part of this exhibition. If we can prompt empathy through the display and get visitors to consider the lives and experiences of others, it will have been a success. The themes that the Heart Mountain Interpretive Center presents are more relevant than ever, which is one of the reasons I think the museum resonates so deeply. I felt a real weight to do right by this exhibition—there's an incredible trust that comes with someone handing their story over to you to share.

## *The Power of Children: Making a Difference* Exhibition, The Children's Museum of Indianapolis, Indianapolis, Indiana[9]

*The Power of Children: Making a Difference* exhibition features immersive storytelling spaces and components, dynamic environments, and live theater that focus upon the achievements of three extraordinary children who touched the world in unique ways: Anne Frank, Ruby Bridges, and Ryan White. Planning and visitor evaluation were key to defining and developing the experience of this potentially sensitive topic aimed at children and families.

### Planning

Founded in 1925, The Children's Museum of Indianapolis is committed to creating extraordinary learning experiences that cut across the arts, sciences, and humanities and have the power to transform the lives of children and families. It is the largest children's museum in the world. This exhibition, which opened in 2007, marked the culmination of five years of planning and development that began with an inquiry from Jeanne White-Ginder, the mother of Ryan White—the Indiana teenager who became internationally known during the early 1980s when he contracted HIV/AIDS. Conversations led to a larger concept: a gallery devoted to telling the story of three courageous children—Ryan White, Anne Frank (whose World War II–era story had already been presented in several temporary exhibitions), and Ruby Bridges (one of the first African American children to attend a previously white-only elementary school in Louisiana).

The main goal of the exhibition was "To create a family learning experience that presents the unique stories of three extraordinary children from history, inspiring people of all ages to create positive change within their own families, schools and communities." It is designed as a safe place for families and students to explore issues of intolerance, fear, and prejudice as experienced in the lives of these three children.

The target audiences for *The Power of Children: Making a Difference* were families with children ages eight and older as well as school groups from grades three through seven.

Early on, members of the core exhibit planning team conducted focus groups with teachers, schoolchildren, and families to assess their familiarity with the three children who were to be featured. After these initial focus groups, twenty families with children in the target age range volunteered to meet on a monthly basis for six months to provide feedback on exhibit content. Dubbed the "Power Families," they included adults and children that tested prototypes for the Anne, Ruby, and Ryan activities. Data from these sessions was used to fine-tune the activities to meet the intended outcomes.

In addition to the formative testing with the Power Families, testing was also conducted in the Museum with random families accompanied by children in the target age range on successive iterations of the prototypes, reactions to selected artifacts (e.g., Nazi objects with swastikas), and label phrasing and content.

## Research

The core exhibit team met with expert advisers and strategic partners to learn from them about the specific stories of the children in the exhibition, to understand how to recreate and enliven the environments, and to receive guidance in the best methods for presenting controversial and difficult topics for families with children. The advisers' historical research was reframed into a "Storyline" for each exhibit area, including direct quotes from historical sources or oral interviews with the living figures in the stories that were woven into the narrative.

## Furnishings and Interpretation

Reproductions and period vintage objects were incorporated into the immersive spaces as hands-on objects or when authentic objects referenced in the stories were unavailable.

The historical environments in *The Power of Children: Making a Difference* serve three functions. First, they recreate the "safe spaces" or sanctuaries in the lives of these real people: Anne Frank's room in the secret annex, Ruby Bridges's classroom at her school, and Ryan White's bedroom at his new home in Cicero, Indiana. As such, the furnishings plans for each story incorporated authentic artifacts and reproductions that allow visitors to suspend disbelief and be transported to the time and place of the story, and understand why the space was a safe haven for the child and her/his helpers.

**Figure 7.3.** An actor interpreter portrays Ryan White for an audience inside the re-creation of Ryan's bedroom in *The Power of Children: Making a Difference* exhibition. The actual contents from Ryan's room can be seen in the background (DSC_2843.jpg).
Photo courtesy of The Children's Museum of Indianapolis

Second, the environments serve as "Voices of Hope" Theater Spaces. These can be temporarily closed off from the rest of the exhibit while costumed professional actors present live theatrical performances to visitors. As such, the furnishings plan and design for each story allow for entry and exit of an actor, doors that close off the space, theatrical lighting, flexible-configuration visitor seating, and a stage of sorts for performance. As scripts were developed for these theatrical performances, a list of furnishings and props that were key to the stories and could be used in the performances was included in the artifact list for each area (see Figure 7.3).

Third, when the spaces are open to general public viewing, they incorporate a variety of audiovisual presentations, ranging from ambient sounds to short (five- to six-minute) sound-and-light shows based upon the storylines. These use dramatic lighting to feature objects and displays within each recreated space that is sequenced to video projected on creatively placed screens, utilizing stock video footage and new images to emphasize the storylines. As such, each recreated environment incorporates theatrical lighting, video projectors, and projection screens. As scripts for these audiovisual presentations were developed, a list of furnishings and props that were key to the stories and could be highlighted with dramatic lighting was included in the artifact list for each area.

Authentic artifacts that help to explain both what was happening at the time of the story and the impact that each child had on society are displayed in traditional cases outside the entrances and exits of each historical environment.

## Relevance and Impact

Both remedial and in-depth summative evaluations were completed for this exhibition. The findings from these evaluations have revealed several positive outcomes, including that *The Power of Children* exhibition encourages word-of-mouth publicity and high repeat visitation; the Museum has succeeded in presenting serious topics in ways that families can approach them at levels of their own choosing; while the strongest impact is among families with children in the target age range, there are also young children (approximately four to five years old) who show comfort with the content and display empathetic responses to parents' explanations of it; and there is consistent evidence of carryover from the exhibition to home in the form of family discussions, continued questions asked by children, and reported instances of "taking action." In addition, the majority of unsolicited comments that have been sent directly to the Museum, as well as those posted online and in blog posts and those made by staff working in the exhibition, are uniformly positive and often effusive.

Christian Carron, director of Collections, believes that "the most memorable thing for visitors to our environments is the encounter with live actor interpreters." Carron adds that the "simple surroundings and props but powerful monologues . . . hold people spellbound. They bring life to the environment, and emotion to the facts of the story." Because the stories are so powerful, the actor interpreters step out of character after the performances to engage in conversation with participants. Carron explains that "This time for processing and for personal reflection and discussion is crucial when addressing sensitive topics, and the whole experience leaves a strong and lasting impression on those who take part."

Carron believes that the stories told in *The Power of Children* historical environments are easily relatable to children. Sadly, the types of racism, discrimination, and hatred that are addressed here are still prevalent in our society today. The success of this exhibition has emboldened the institution to tackle other experiences that are focused upon cultural awareness and tolerance.

## "Get to the Basement!" Story Theater in the *Weather Permitting* Exhibition, Minnesota History Center, St. Paul, Minnesota[10]

This immersive media experience inside a recreated basement environment places visitors in the shoes of those who waited out a fierce tornado that battered Findley, Minnesota, in 1965. It is a groundbreaking example of how theatrical techniques allow visitors to enter the scene and become part of the story.

## Planning

With twenty-six historic sites and its flagship History Center, the Minnesota Historical Society has become one of the most prestigious historical societies in the country. Since the Minnesota History Center museum building opened in 1992, the staff has looked to the potential of telling stories through immersive media that resonate with audiences. These use personal stories, a strong narrative arc, the audience's own desire to suspend disbelief, and advances in automated, computer-based show systems being developed in theater and the theme park industry. The first of these so-called Story Theatre experiences was "Home Place Minnesota," an enclosed fifty-seat story and object theater experience that used multichannel sound (multi-image, twelve-slide projectors), hide-and-reveal techniques, and a synchronized show control system to evoke in the audience the visceral longing for home.

As the staff developed subsequent experiences, they worked to enhance the prospect of immersion experiences that erased the line between viewers and the experience, likening this to the viewer actually stepping onstage and becoming part of the drama. This, they posited, not only would create an experience unique to their museum visit but it "takes as a departure point the visitor's natural proclivities to discover exhibit content at a leisurely and self-directed pace."[11] "Get to the Basement!"—developed in 2002—was the first of these experiences, providing the model for truly breaking out of the black box of a traditional sit-down formal theater to a seamlessly integrated component of an exhibit gallery. This experience also draws upon audience research findings at the Minnesota Historical Society that museum visitors most readily connect to history through the personal stories of others.

## Research

The accounts conveyed in this experience came from actual news clips and mass media coverage of the 1965 Findley, Minnesota, tornado, as well as the personal accounts of a focus group of community members.

*Furnishings and Interpretation*

The story of the tornado informed both the overall space and its furnish-ings. Most of the furnishings are actual objects from the era but they are often treated as touchable props in the space. For example, the television becomes basically a shell for a series of film clips, while ordinary household tools and other items of the era are bolted to the wall and worktable. The space itself is a recreation, designed to incorporate directed lighting, show controls, and a vibrating apparatus built into the benches for visitor seating.

As with other story theater experiences at the Minnesota Historical Soci-ety, this involved prototyping at an off-site warehouse. Rough cardboard pro-totypes of the show, space, and story were quickly created, to get the concept down and inform the design. These were then refined as they were tested. According to Jesse Heinzen, multimedia director, the prototyping process for this experience was "collaborative, iterative, and self-correcting."

Out of this prototyping phase emerged a theatrical simulation of the disas-trous sequence of events that occurred in Findley, Minnesota, in 1965, inside an enclosed space in the *Weather Permitting* exhibition. Before visitors enter this space, they are clued in to what's ahead through a recreated scene of the upper floor of the house that seems to be ripped away as well as an interpre-tive label that explains the events that occurred (see Figure 1.3). During peak visitation, gallery interpreters help orient visitors and start the show. At other times, the show can be started directly by visitors. As visitors "seek shelter" in the basement of the house, the "tornado" is conveyed through a series of multisensory clues: lighting, ambient sounds like crashing thunder and a tree falling outside the basement window, the feeling that the floor is shaking, a news broadcast on the radio, and personal reminiscences combined with actual news footage on the television.

*Relevance and Impact*

Although dramatic and multisensory effects provide clues to the story, in the end, much is left to the imagination. And that, to the creators of this ex-perience, is the key to the powerful and memorable quality of story theater. As Michael Mouw and Daniel Spock wrote in their essay, "Immersive Media: Creating Theatrical Storytelling Experiences":

> Stories that reach the essence of the human experience and can be dramatized in such ways that visitors feel a close sense of connection to the story physically, emotionally and cognitively have the most impact and leave the most durable impression. For visitors, this is fundamentally an act of the imagination.[12]

This experience has influenced the creation of similar experiences in other museums, including the Tornado Alley Theater at the Museum of Discovery in Little Rock, Arkansas, and the Dust Bowl experience at History Colorado.

## *You Are There* Exhibit Galleries, Indiana Historical Society, Indianapolis, Indiana[13]

This series of changing exhibits in three galleries at the Indiana Historical Society is a superb success story arising out of strategic planning and a recognized need for institutional transformation. Each of the *You Are There* exhibits uses the basic premise of visitor time travel (i.e., visitors "step through" a photograph or document and cross a portal that transports them to a particular moment in history). In each of these *You Are There* galleries, visitors interact with two to three actors whose characters are in, or associated with, the image or document being used.

### *Planning*

The Indiana Historical Society was established in 1830, devoted to "collecting, preserving, interpreting, and disseminating the history of the Old Northwest Territory and Indiana." The collections are primarily library and archival, including over 1.7 million historical photographs. In 2006, the Historical Society engaged in a critical analysis of its strengths, weaknesses, mission, and programs, in a concerted effort to explore ways to remain relevant. This analysis resulted in a plan to create a series of new visitor experiences that would both provide visitors with more personalized experiences and foster within them a deeper understanding and appreciation of Indiana history.

President and CEO John Herbst (now retired) encouraged the development team to use the institution's assets to create lively, engaging experiences that would make its archival collections accessible in a unique way. From focus group interviews and other formal evaluation techniques, the Historical Society learned that people examining historical photographs often expressed the wish that they could go back in time to explore that moment in history. At the same time, the Historical Society realized that it had relatively small galleries to work with and needed to design a changing exhibit program that could bring members and visitors back several times a year. These realizations led to the *You Are There* exhibit galleries, a changing series of immersive experiences that recreates scenes from historic photographs and documents through the use of three-dimensional environments and first-person interpreters. These vary in location, year, and topics as much as possible—thus far, ranging in date from 1816 to 1968.

*Research*

Historical research for each photograph or document—undertaken by staff members or outside researchers—leads to a written white paper, which serves as the "interpretive bible" for everyone involved with the exhibit, including interpreters, facilitators, public relations staff, and development staff.

*Furnishings and Interpretation*

The research provides the framework for a narrative that is based upon the date of the photograph or document. A likely date is assigned if the image or document does not have a precise one. Character profiles and biographical narratives are created for the actors who will be assuming the roles of people related to each photograph or document.

When photographs are selected, they are used to replicate the space. When documents are used, an appropriate interior is created after additional research is completed. A combination of artifacts lacking provenance and reproductions is used to furnish each gallery so that actors and visitors have access to everything. In each of the galleries, visitors "step into" a photograph or document projected on mist and when they emerge on the other side of the mist, they feel as if they have been transported back to the moment of time of the archival piece through the faithfully recreated environment (see Figure 1.5).

According to Dr. David D. Vail, in his *Public History* review of the *Eli Lilly at the Beginning* exhibit (*You Are There 1939: Healing Bodies, Changing Minds*), the interpreters in the galleries receive "exceptional training" from Dan Shockley, the Historical Society's Director of Museum Theater.[14] Gearing their presentation toward each visitor's interest, they bring dimension to the characters they portray as well as to "the period's critical scholarship and primary sources."[15] This particular exhibit also linked science, technology, engineering, and math (STEM) fields with humanities interpretation in experiential ways (see Figure 7.4).

School and youth groups receive a specially tailored presentation in the *You Are There* galleries because of their limited time and the teachers' own content goals.

All *You Are There* experiences also include a traditional exhibition that provides context before and after the first-person encounters. Visitors are briefed by trained facilitators who explain the time frame of the scene, characters they will encounter, and activities in which they can engage in the immersive space. The facilitators also suggest questions that visitors can ask the interpreters in the space. This has helped make the first-person experience less daunting.

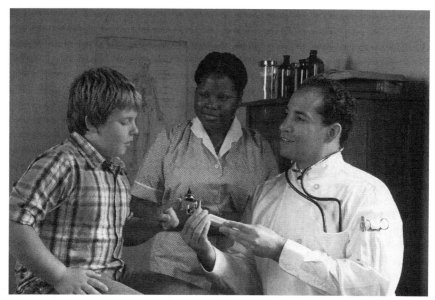

**Figure 7.4.** **A scene from the *You Are There 1939: Healing Bodies, Changing Minds* exhibit at Indiana Historical Society, showing a young visitor interacting with first-person interpreters.**
Courtesy of the Indiana Historical Society

For the eighteen months that each *You Are There* exhibit is open to the public, the Museum has encountered few problems with the environments holding up.

## Relevance and Impact

Visitor evaluations show a high level of satisfaction and high marks for believability, authenticity, and effective methods of historical presentation. One visitor went so far as to state that, "Without a doubt, the changes . . . to the [Indiana] Historical Society building have turned the presentation of history upside down!" As John Herbst and Trina Nelson Thomas wrote in their article, "The Power of Personal Connections," the *You Are There* exhibits "are terrific vehicles for sharing collections with a broader public and are helping people understand Indiana Historical Society's central role of preserving historical photographs and archival materials."[16]

Since the 2010 opening of the *You Are There* galleries, the public's sense of the Historical Society as a cultural destination has grown significantly, and the overall *Indiana Experience*—of which these galleries are a part—has resulted in increased membership, community visibility, financial support, and attendance. In his exemplary review of these galleries, Dr. Vail remarked that "*You Are There* stands as a prototype for future immersive exhibitions. It weaves local, regional, and national histories together in ways that serve as a compelling model of interdisciplinary public history."[17]

## ENVIRONMENTS IN HISTORIC STRUCTURES

### La Tiendita, El Rancho de las Golondrinas, Santa Fe, New Mexico[18]

La Tiendita (the "little store") is an example of a modest interpretive program at a historic site that has had great impact.

*Planning*

El Rancho de las Golondrinas is a living history museum located on 200 acres in a rural farming valley just south of Santa Fe, New Mexico, with its mission to "inspire learning and preserve the legacy of the land through encounters with the traditions and culture of New Mexico's Hispano past." This 1890 store was brought to the Las Golondrinas site from Las Trampas, New Mexico, located high in the Sierras between Santa Fe and Taos, and operated as a general store and post office until 1940. In planning the interpretation for the store, museum staff members wanted visitors to actively engage in trade and barter—key concepts of early commerce in New Mexico. The experience would be geared toward visitors of all ages, but it targeted school-age children, especially fourth graders who attend the Museum's annual Spanish Colonial Days event.

*Research*

The research sources consulted for this store included property descriptions of local inhabitants of the time; lists of material coming to Santa Fe by wagon and train; local mercantile listings and accounts; mail-order catalogs of the era; source material from the collections of Las Golondrinas and other museums; and firsthand accounts of general stores in New Mexico.

*Furnishings and Interpretation*

Based upon the historical research, the store was furnished with objects that were specific to rural New Mexican general stores. Most of these were actual artifacts that came from the Museum's collections. Reproductions were planned for items that would be sold or bartered.

The primary interpretive technique at the store is the bartering interaction that occurs between visitors and the volunteers who staff the building. Teachers are encouraged to have their classes come prepared to barter at the Spanish Colonial Days event. Modern reproduction items related to the era can actually be purchased at the store, such as wooden tops, jacks, wrought iron scissors, fur pelts, and trade beads (see Figure 1.1).

### Relevance and Impact

Daniel Goodman, Museum director, feels that the store's greatest impact on visitors is the power of the historic structure and the artifacts within it. The relevance of this experience to visitors, Goodman believes, is that there is "an inherent interest in consumer goods from the past." Shopping, he adds, is "very accessible to everyone; it's an easy bridge to get guests engaged with the past." Goodman is particularly proud of the volunteers who interpret the space and interact with visitors, remarking that, "They have taken ownership of the exhibit and take great pride in their interactions with visitors. Having an authentic space has allowed them to move their interpretation to the next level."

## 1864 Governors' Mansion, Sharlot Hall Museum, Prescott, Arizona[19]

The personal papers of a past inhabitant of this historic structure revealed details about living here that greatly enhanced its interpretation.

### Planning

The four-acre Sharlot Hall Museum is a heritage site with eleven exhibit buildings, six of which are historic. The 1864 Governors' Mansion is the oldest building associated with the Arizona Territory still standing on its original location and the first building to be used by the Museum's founder, Sharlot M. Hall, as a place to exhibit artifacts.

A grant to restore this historic structure and the subsequent removal of exhibited artifacts from it offered a prime opportunity to re-envision it, focusing upon the era in which it was home to the first two governors of the Territory. Museum staff members wanted visitors here to gain a better understanding of the difficulties that the first Arizona territorial officers encountered when trying to set up a new government in the wilderness.

### Research

Initial research included oral histories collected by the Museum's founder; newspaper articles of the establishment of Prescott as the first territorial capital; and an archaeological survey of the floor area of each room that recovered artifacts confirming room use. Several years later, the Museum began receiving material that related to the second governor's wife, including a diary and several letters that she had written back home expressing her personal feelings about living here. One of these also included a complete description of the building and its contents. These letters and this journal offered a unique window into these spaces, allowing museum staff to refine a narrative for each room that was more personal and authentic.

## Furnishings and Interpretation

The furnished rooms reveal a mixture of "make do" and affluence of the original occupants. In a room staffed by a docent, a more traditional exhibit reveals how the building was constructed—showcasing original tools, building techniques, and a sampling of original artifacts recovered from the archaeology of the floor areas. In addition, a room that was designated as a spare bedroom in the original letters has been turned into an interactive "Frontier Discovery Room," in which visitors can lift the lids of containers to see objects up close that are far away in the room settings.

## Relevance and Impact

Mick Woodcock, chief curator of Sharlot Hall Museum, feels that, even though this imposing log structure was once a mansion inhabited by government officials, visitors can personally connect with the idea that "We all occupy dwelling spaces. This is a more primitive version of what people have today. People can relate to having to 'make do' as well as having a few good objects that they treasure."

## 1930s George Ranch Home, George Ranch Historical Park, Richmond, Texas[20]

Since 1988, the 1930s-era ranch home of Mamie and A. P. George has served as the proud centerpiece of a 480-acre living history site (on their 23,000-acre ranch) that showcases the ranching heritage of Texas. Over time, museum staff has refined, modified, and incorporated new material and program elements into the traditional tour format to meet the needs of current audiences. Like many historic house installations, this is a work in progress.

## Introduction

In 1988, the Board of Trustees of the George Foundation resolved to open a living history site to preserve the original homestead and provide a glimpse into four generations of the family who worked this extensive and prosperous ranching operation. Partnering with the Fort Bend History Association, the Foundation's and Association's efforts resulted in a nationally prominent historic site showcasing the heritage of Texas over four eras. The most recent of these—the 1930s George Ranch Home—is still standing where it was built at the turn of the century and filled with many original furnishings of Mamie George, the last descendant of the original homesteaders to oversee the ranching operation with her husband Albert.

## Research and Furnishings

The late 1930s to early 1940s period was chosen to represent the time during which Mamie and A. P. were in good health and the ranch was a hub of activity. Painstaking historical research was undertaken to reflect the essence of the Georges' tastes and personalities, including an in-depth study of the structure and a room-by-room assessment of appropriate furnishings and floor and wall coverings. Blueprints of the house revealed details of the layout and architectural features from the original 1899 plan and a 1911 remodeling. Oral history interviews with several individuals who had known the Georges and visited the house while they lived there filled in many of the details of room use and furnishings arrangement. Exterior photographs, receipts from purchases of interior features, and correspondence mentioning work done on the house were also uncovered in the Park archives and provided clues to the house and its furnishings. In furnishing the rooms, Mamie George's personality was particularly revealed through the displays of boots that can be found throughout the house which she had collected during her travels.

## Interpretation and Refinements

Interpreters take visitors through the home on guided tours, focused upon revealing aspects of the Georges' tastes and personalities. The staff continually incorporates new material into the tour narratives where they can. The overall narrative has been reworked several times, and changes are still being made based upon new information that becomes available. New mini-exhibits are often created in the home and objects are added or switched out as needed.

The staff also recognizes that times have changed and visitors are looking for more. Staff members are constantly looking at current programs and modifying them to meet the needs and expectations of current audiences. For example, living history tours with first-person role-players in period clothing have been added for special events like the Association's Texian Market Days Festival. Hands-on activities occur on the porch on certain occasions.

To move beyond the story of the ranch owners Mamie and A. P., the staff is actively looking to tell the stories of longtime workers at the ranch as well. Staff is also trying to figure out how to incorporate modern technology into the experience to showcase period images and film in a way that will not distract from the period setting.

### *Relevance and Impact*

Museum staff believes that visitors make many connections here with their own lives. Although the ranch home and its furnishings are specific to the Georges, the rooms, objects, and activities that would have taken place here are familiar and relatable. Staff also believes that this site is relevant and significant for school-age audiences. Krystal Willeby, director of programs, remarks that

> With the recent thought process of schools trying to reduce history from the curriculum, we are seeing a number of kids coming to the Park with no understanding of the past. By bringing the past alive and teaching it in a way that is engaging to them, they can appreciate it. Hopefully this new understanding will stir in them the desire to continue learning about history on their own after they have finished their visit. This is not just the history of one family but the history of all of us in general.

### Charles Lindbergh House and Museum, Little Falls, Minnesota[21]

A unique aspect of the interpretation of this historic structure is the role of an exhibit enhancement to expand upon a key story that took place in the attic of the house—a space inaccessible to visitors.

### *Introduction*

Four years after Charles Lindbergh's childhood home was heavily damaged by souvenir seekers when the young flyer became a worldwide celebrity in 1927, the Lindbergh family made the decision to give the farmhouse and the 110-acre surrounding site on the banks of the Mississippi River to the state of Minnesota. During the 1930s and over the next several decades, the house was restored and returned to its 1906–1920 appearance—the years in which the family had lived there. In 1969, the Minnesota Historical Society took over the management of the house and seventeen acres of the larger State Park to preserve and interpret the Lindbergh family history during that era. A Museum adjacent to the house, which opened in 1973, tells the fuller story of Charles Lindbergh's life and impact on our society.

*Research and Furnishings*

During the late 1960s and early 1970s, Lindbergh himself had advised on the furnishings and arrangement in the house as well as consulting on the exhibits in the Museum. His eighty-five-page handwritten reminiscence about life on this farm, "Boyhood on the Upper Mississippi: A Reminiscent Letter," aided with this effort. As Minnesota Historical Society curator (now retired) Brian Horrigan remarked in his article, "'My Own Mind and Pen': Charles Lindbergh, Autobiography, and Memory," this was "an extraordinary relationship between a historical organization and a living figure stepping out of the pages of history."[22] The house became, in essence, "a virtual autobiography in three dimensions."[23] Lindbergh's personal involvement and the fact that over 90 percent of the furnishings in the home are original greatly adds to the authenticity of the site. Staff members working on later upgrades and refinements also consulted the numerous existing published materials on Lindbergh, along with his papers at Yale University.

*Interpretation of the Charles Lindbergh House*

Guided tours of Lindbergh's boyhood home include stories of Lindbergh's life that are not as well known as the usual stories of his famous flight and his celebrity status afterward. When visiting the home, visitors have the opportunity to see a more intimate picture of Lindbergh's childhood—a time that shaped the character, interests, and values of the man he would become. As Melissa Peterson, site manager at the Charles Lindbergh House and Museum, remarks, "There are no barriers. We also don't have red velvet ropes. So you're walking through his house and I think that helps you get a good idea of what it was like to grow up on a farm in central Minnesota almost 100 years ago."[24]

In 2002, as part of a systematic plan to enhance the exhibits at Minnesota Historical Society sites, a project team developed a series of upgraded exhibits at the Museum next to Lindbergh's childhood home. School-age audiences were particularly targeted, though the needs and interests of tourists and Lindbergh enthusiasts were also considered. A primary goal for these enhancements was to find fun, engaging ways to get across both the factors that shaped Lindbergh as a child growing up on this farm and his ultimate place in history.

The idea of recreating an attic environment emerged out of a pivotal moment that occurred in young Charles's life, a moment that seemed to perfectly blend these two topics together. According to the story that Lindbergh himself conveyed, he was playing in the attic one day, heard the sound of an unusual engine outside, climbed out the attic window onto the roof to get a better look, and saw an airplane for the first time. As the tight stairs and ADA requirements prevent visitors from gaining access to the actual attic in the

**Figure 7.5.** Design rendering of the recreated attic environment at the Charles Lindbergh House and Museum, Little Falls, Minnesota. This immersive space contains Lindbergh's original toys, an audio of his reminiscences, interpretive labels, and an attic eave-like structure (on the right side) through which young visitors can crawl.
Courtesy of Brad Thiel

house, recreating the space as accurately as possible in the Museum became an intriguing alternative (see Figure 7.5).

In this faithfully recreated environment, visitors can hear Lindbergh's reminiscences about playing in the attic and see his actual toys, arranged as he would have played with them as a boy. Then, young visitors can crawl under an attic eave and pretend to be young Lindbergh himself. Brad Thiel, exhibit designer (now retired) for the immersive attic space, feels that "By allowing young children to crawl under the eave and see all the toys from a kids' eye view, we hoped that they would make a connection between their own lives and that of young Charles." This "pretend play," he believes, is "crucial to creating memories for the people who visit." In this way, the immersive attic environment not only recreates an inaccessible space in the house but also provides a memorable, emotionally resonant, and enjoyable experience of its own.

## COMING FULL CIRCLE

Assessing connections between these examples brings us full circle back to chapters 1 and 2 of *Spaces That Tell Stories: Recreating Historical Environments*. Not surprisingly, the value and impact of these examples closely align with the benefits of historical environments as laid out in chapter 1, including learning through active engagement, emotional impact, memory retention, personal meaning-making, enhanced social experiences, and indications of increased empathy for others. Moreover, many of the successful strategies described here also reach back to those laid out by the pioneers of historical environments described in chapter 2, including having a unified and coherent vision, insisting upon a scrupulous attention to detail, infusing spaces with the presence of people, and inviting visitors to become active participants in the experience. Several times in these examples, specific phases of planning, research, implementation, and refinement (as described in chapters 3 through 6) were called out as crucial to ensuring visitor focus and engagement, institutional alignment, historical accuracy, and long-term maintenance and durability. Furthermore, when connected with an institution's mission, vision, and strategic goals, these environments can lead to such rewards as increased attendance, repeat visitation, membership growth, positive word of mouth and "buzz," enhanced community engagement, and financial support—in short, many of the building blocks that ensure museums' continued relevance and long-term sustainability.

## NOTES

1. The following sources were referenced for this write-up: Michelle Moon, email correspondence, October 9, 2018; the Tenement Museum website, accessed September 23, 2018, https://www.tenement.org/; Ellysheva Zeira, "Accessibility at the Tenement Museum" (blog), July 19, 2016, https://tenement.org/blog/accessibility-at -the-tenement-museum/; Rebecca Truchman, "Shop Life: Review of an Exhibition," ASTC (Association of Science-Technology Centers) ExhibitFiles website, April 9, 2013, accessed September 18, 2018, http://www.exhibitfiles.org/shop_life; and Erin Cabrey, "Tenement Museum Recreates the Life of Three Immigrant Families in New York City Exhibit 'Under One Roof,'" Untapped Cities website, September 29, 2017, accessed September 18, 2018, https://untappedcities.com/2017/09/29/tenement-mu seum-recreates-the-lives-of-3-immigrant-families-in-nyc-exhibition-under-one -roof/. For other sources related to The Tenement Museum, see Stuart Miller, *A Tenement Story: The History of 97 Orchard Street and the Lower East Side Tenement Museum* (New York: Lower East Side Tenement Museum, 2014); Linda Granfield and Arlene Alda, *97 Orchard Street, New York: Stories of Immigrant Life* (Plattsburgh, New York: Lower East Side Tenement Museum and Tundra Books of Northern New York, 2001); Adam P. Nilsen and Miriam Bader, "The Psychology

of Empathy: Compelling Possibilities for Museums," in *Fostering Empathy through Museums*, ed. Elif M. Gokcigdem (Lanham, MD: Rowman & Littlefield, 2016), 115–29; and Dara Horn, "The Tenement Museum," *American Heritage* 51, no. 2 (April 2000), American Heritage website, accessed September 23, 2018, https://www.americanheritage.com/content/tenement-museum.

2. Russell A. Kazal, "Migration History in Five Stories (and a Basement): The Lower East Side Tenement Museum," *Journal of American Ethnic History* 34, no. 4 (Summer 2015): 77.

3. The following sources were referenced for this write-up: Benjamin Filene, "Hearing Voices in 'Open House: If These Walls Could Talk,'" *History News* 63, no. 2 (Spring 2008): 19–23; Filene, "Make Yourself at Home—Welcoming Voices in *Open House: If These Walls Could Talk*," in *Letting Go? Sharing Historical Authority in a User-Generated World*, ed. Bill Adair, Benjamin Filene, and Laura Koloski (Philadelphia: The Pew Center for Arts and Heritage, 2011), 138–55; Filene, "Are We There Yet? Children, History, and the Power of Place," in *Connecting Kids to History with Museum Exhibitions*, ed. D. Lynn McRainey and John Russick (Walnut Creek, CA: Left Coast Press, 2010), 173–95; and the Minnesota Historical Society website, accessed September 23, 2018, https://www.mnhs.org.

4. Filene, "Make Yourself at Home," 140.

5. Ibid., 139.

6. This section is based upon comments from Megan Wood and Bill Mahon, email response to questionnaire provided by author, May 21, 2018. Additional background information was drawn from the Ohio History Connection website, accessed July 23, 2018, https://www.ohiohistory.org/.

7. This section is based upon comments from Christopher K. Wilson, telephone interview in response to questionnaire provided by author, May 23, 2018; subsequent email correspondence, September 20, 2018, and September 24, 2018; Sarah Bartlett, email correspondence, September 26, 2018; and the Heart Mountain Interpretive Center, Heart Mountain Foundation website, accessed July 23, 2018, http://www.heartmountain.org/.

8. "Excellence in Exhibition Competition," *Museum* 91, no. 6 (November–December 2012): 39.

9. This section is based upon comments from Christian G. Carron and Jennifer Pace Robinson, email response to questionnaire provided by author, May 23, 2018. Additional background information was drawn from The Children's Museum of Indianapolis website, accessed July 23, 2018, https://www.childrensmuseum.org/.

10. This section is based upon comments from Jesse Heinzen, in-person interview in response to questionnaire provided by author, June 15, 2018. Additional background information was drawn from the Minnesota Historical Society website, accessed July 23, 2018, https://www.mnhs.org/.

11. Michael Mouw and Daniel Spock, *The Digital Museum: A Think Guide*, ed. Herminia Din and Phyllis Hecht (Washington, DC: American Association of Museums, 2007), 52.

12. Ibid., 55.

13. This section is based upon comments from John Herbst, email response to questionnaire provided by author, June 6, 2018. Additional background information was drawn from Herbst and Trina Nelson Thomas, "The Power of Personal Connections," *History News* 67, no. 2 (Spring 2012): 17–20; and Herbst, "Indiana Historical Society: A Summary Background on the Developing of the *Indiana Experience*" (unpublished manuscript prepared for the Seminar for Historical Administration, November 14, 2017).

14. "Review of *You Are There: Eli Lilly at the Beginning*," *The Public Historian*, 39, no. 3 (August 2017): 114.

15. Ibid.

16. Herbst and Thomas, "The Power of Personal Connections," 19.

17. Vail, "Review of *You Are There: Eli Lilly at the Beginning*," 115.

18. This section is based upon comments from Daniel Goodman, email response to questionnaire provided by author, May 21, 2018. Additional background information was drawn from the Las Golondrinas website, accessed July 23, 2018, https://golondrinas.org/.

19. This section is based upon comments from Mick Woodcock, email response to questionnaire provided by author, June 15, 2018. Additional background information was drawn from the Sharlot Hall Museum website, accessed July 23, 2018, https://www.sharlot.org/.

20. This section is based upon comments from Krystal Willeby, Matt Driggers, and Chris Godbold, email response to questionnaire provided by author, August 20, 2018. Additional background information was drawn from the George Ranch website, accessed September 2, 2018, https://www.georgeranch.org/; and "Interior Restoration of the A. P. George Ranch, Arroyo Seco Historical Park, Richmond, Texas" (unpublished report, March 28, 1986).

21. This section is based upon comments from Brad Thiel, email response to questionnaire provided by author, August 31, 2018; subsequent email correspondence, September 11, 2018, and September 12, 2018, and telephone interview, September 20, 2018; and Melissa Peterson, email correspondence, September 23, 2018. Additional background information was drawn from the Charles Lindbergh House and Museum on Minnesota Historical Society website, accessed September 2, 2018, http://www.mnhs.org/lindbergh; and "Charles A. Lindbergh House," Spirit of St. Louis 2 website, 2014, accessed September 2, 2018, http://www.charleslindbergh.com/house/outside/outside1outsi.asp.

22. *Minnesota History* 58, no. 4 (Spring 2002): 13.

23. Ibid.

24. "Charles A. Lindbergh House," AM 1240 WJON YouTube video, February 18, 2014, accessed September 2, 2018, https://www.youtube.com/watch?v=YsthrZ3J24I.

# Bibliography

"The 20th Century Exhibit Project Plan." Unpublished manuscript, 9 November 1998. Braden Papers.

Alderson, William T., and Shirley Payne Low. *Interpretation of Historic Sites*. 2nd ed. Walnut Creek, CA: AltaMira Press, 1996.

Allison, David B. *Living History: Effective Costumed Interpretation and Enactment at Museums and Historic Sites*. Lanham, MD: Rowman & Littlefield, 2016.

American Alliance of Museums. "Museums and Accessibility." *Museum* (entire issue) 94, no. 5 (September/October 2015).

Ames, Kenneth L. "Meaning in Artifacts: Hall Furnishings in Victorian America." *Journal of Interdisciplinary History* 9 (Summer 1978): 19–46.

Ames, Kenneth L., Barbara Franco, and L. Thomas Frye, eds. *Ideas and Images: Developing Interpretive History Exhibits*. Nashville, TN: American Association for State and Local History, 1992.

Anderson, Jay. "Living History." In *A Living History Reader*. Vol. 1, *Museums*, edited by Jay Anderson, 3–12. Nashville, TN: American Association for State and Local History, 1991.

———. *Time Machines: The World of Living History*. Nashville, TN: American Association for State and Local History, 1984.

Arp, Thomas R., and Greg Johnson. *Perrine's Story and Structure: An Introduction to Fiction*. 12th ed. Boston, MA: Wadsworth Cengage Learning, 2009.

"Back Story for Commune in *Your Place in Time* Exhibition, Sample Questions." Unpublished manuscript, 27 March 2007. Donna Braden Papers, Benson Ford Research Center, The Henry Ford, Dearborn, MI (hereafter cited as Braden Papers).

"Back to the Land Inventory." Unpublished manuscript, n.d., ca. 1999. Braden Papers.

Baker, Andrew, and Warren Leon. "Old Sturbridge Village Introduces Social Conflict into Its Interpretive Story." In *A Living History Reader*. Vol. 1, *Museums*, edited by Jay Anderson, 110–18. Nashville, TN: American Association for State and Local History, 1991.

Baker, James W. "Looking Back—Looking Forward—Looking Around." *Proceedings of the 1990 Annual Meeting, Providence, Rhode Island*, edited by Debra Reid and Ken Yellis. Vol. XIII (Santa Fe, NM: The Association for Living Historical Farms and Agricultural Museums, 1993), 12–18.

———. "World View at Plimoth Plantation: History and Theory." *Proceedings of the 1990 Annual Meeting, Providence, Rhode Island*, edited by Debra Reid and Ken Yellis. Vol. XIII (Santa Fe, NM: The Association for Living Historical Farms and Agricultural Museums, 1993), 64–67.

Barnes, Christine. *Hopi House: Celebrating 100 Years*. Bend, OR: W.W. West, 2005.

Bauer, Marion Dune. *What's Your Story? A Young Person's Guide to Writing Fiction*. New York: Clarion Books, 1992.

Beard, Colin, and John P. Wilson. *Experiential Learning: A Handbook for Education, Training and Coaching*. 3rd ed. London: Kogan Page, 2013.

Bell, Paul A., Jeffrey D. Fisher, Andrew Baum, Thomas C. Greene. *Environmental Psychology*. 3rd ed. Fort Worth, TX: Holt Rinehart and Winston, 1990.

Bedford, Leslie. *The Art of Museum Exhibitions: How Story and Imagination Create Aesthetic Experiences*. Walnut Creek, CA: Left Coast Press, 2014.

———. "Finding the Story in History." In *Connecting Kids to History with Museum Exhibitions*, edited by D. Lynn McRainey and John Russick, 97–116. Walnut Creek, CA: Left Coast Press, 2010.

———. "Storytelling: The Real Work of Museums." *Curator* 44, no. 1 (January 2001): 27–34.

———. "Working in the Subjunctive Mood: Imagination and Museums." *Curator* 47, no. 1 (January 2004): 5–11.

Berke, Arnold. *Mary Colter: Architect of the Southwest*. New York: Princeton Architectural Press, 2002.

Bitgood, Stephen. *Attention and Value: Keys to Understanding Museum Visitors*. Walnut Creek, CA: Left Coast Press, 2013.

———. *Engaging the Visitor: Designing Exhibits That Work*. Edinburgh: Museums-Etc, 2014.

Bitgood, Stephen, and Harris Shettel. "Remedial Evaluation: How Do We Improve an Exhibition after Opening?" In *Introduction to Museum Evaluation*, edited by Minda Borun and Randi Korn, 69–86. Washington, DC: American Association of Museums, 1999.

Black, Graham. *The Engaging Museum: Developing Museums for Visitor Involvement*. London: Routledge, 2005.

Bodeman, Dorsey. "Everything Teachers Want to Know about Primary Sources But Are Afraid to Ask." *Proceedings of the 1997 Conference and Annual Meeting, Staunton, Virginia*, edited by Debra A. Reid. Vol. XX (North Bloomfield, OH: The Association for Living Historical Farms and Agricultural Museums, 1998), 212–14.

Bogart, Barbara Allen. "Using Oral History in Museums." *History News* 50, no. 4 (Autumn 1995): Technical Leaflet #191.

Boorstin, Daniel J. *Hidden History: Exploring Our Secret Past*. New York: Vintage Books, a Division of Random House, 1989.

Borun, Minda, and Randi Korn, eds. *Introduction to Museum Evaluation*. Washington, DC: American Association of Museums, 1999.

Braden, Caroline. "Welcoming All Visitors: Museums, Accessibility, and Visitors with Disabilities." *University of Michigan Working Papers in Museum Studies* Number 12 (2016): 3–15. Accessed June 23, 2018. http://ummsp.rackham.umich .edu/wp-content/uploads/2016/10/Braden-working-paper-FINAL-pdf.pdf.

Braden, Donna R. "Exhibition Label Makeovers." Workshop presented at the 2017 Association of Midwest Museums Annual Conference and Meeting, Des Moines, IA, July 2017.

———. "Great Exhibits Don't Happen by Accident." Paper presented with Dean Krimmel at the 2015 American Association for State and Local History Annual Meeting, Louisville, KY, September 2015.

———. "Not Just a Bunch of Facts: Crafting Dynamic Interpretive Manuals." *History News* 69, no. 3 (Summer 2014): Technical Leaflet #267.

———. "The Process and the Product: Transforming the General Store in Greenfield Village." *History News* 50, no. 3 (Summer 1995): 20–24.

———. "Rowing in the Same Direction: Building Collaborative Project Teams." Paper presented with Cynthia Torp at the 2017 Association of Midwest Museums Annual Conference and Meeting, Des Moines, IA, July 2017.

———. "Taste-Testing the Visitor Experience." *Proceedings of the 2013 Conference and Annual Meeting*, Hale Farm & Village, Akron, Ohio, edited by Debra A. Reid. Vol. XXXVI (North Bloomfield, OH: The Association for Living History, Farm and Agricultural Museums, 2014), 197–211.

———. "What Are They Thinking? Visitor-Centered Exhibition Planning." Paper presented with Lorrie Beaumont and Sheila Brommel at the 2016 Association of Midwest Museums Annual Conference and Meeting, Minneapolis, MN, July 2016.

———. "Where to Begin? The First Steps of Exhibition Planning." Workshop presented at the 2016 Association of Midwest Museums Annual Conference and Meeting, Minneapolis, MN, July 2016.

———. "Your Personal Toolkit: Easing through Friction, Fracas, and Free-for-All." *N.A.M.E. Exhibitionist* 29, no. 1 (Spring 2010): 6–14.

Braden, Donna R., and Mary Lynn Heininger. "General Stores: The Process and the Product." *Proceedings of the 1993 Conference and Annual Meeting, St. Paul, Minnesota*, edited by Mary Seelhorst and Susan Gangwere McCabe. Vol. XVI (Santa Fe, NM: The Association for Living Historical Farms and Agricultural Museums, 1994), 42–70.

Bright, Randy. *Disneyland Inside Story*. New York: Henry N. Abrams, 1987.

Brochu, Lisa, and Tim Merriman. *Personal Interpretation: Connecting Your Audience with Heritage Resources*. 2nd ed. Fort Collins, CO: National Association for Interpretation, 2008.

Brooks, Bradley. "The Historic House Furnishings Plan: Process and Product." In *Interpreting Historic House Museums*, edited by Jessica Foy Donnelly, 128–43. Lanham, MD: AltaMira Press, a Division of Rowman & Littlefield, 2002.

Bryk, Nancy E. Villa. "'I Wish You Could Take a Peak at Us in the Present Moment': Infusing the Historic House with Characters and Activity." *Interpreting Historic*

*House Museums*, edited by Jessica Foy Donnelly, 144–67. Lanham, MD: AltaMira Press, a Division of Rowman & Littlefield, 2002.

Burnes, Brian, Robert W. Butler, and Dan Viets. *Walt Disney's Missouri: The Roots of a Creative Genius*. Kansas City, MO: Kansas City Star Books, 2002.

Cameron, Catherine M., and John B. Gatewood. "Excursions into the Unremembered Past: What People Want from Visits to Historic Sites." *The Public Historian* 22, no. 3 (Summer 2000): 107–127.

Carson, Barbara G., and Cary Carson. "Things Unspoken: Learning Social History from Artifacts." In *Ordinary People and Everyday Life: Perspectives on New Social History*, edited by James B. Gardner and George Rollie Adams, 180–203. Nashville, TN: The American Association for State and Local History, 1983.

Carson, Cary. 1978. "Doing History with Material Culture." In *Material Culture and the Study of American Life: A Winterthur Book*, edited by Ian M. G. Quimby, 41–64. New York: W.W. Norton, 1978.

———. 1991. "Living Museums of Everyman's History." In *A Living History Reader*. Vol. 1, *Museums*, edited by Jay Anderson, 25–31. Nashville, TN: American Association for State and Local History, 1991.

Cheney, Theodore A. Rees. *Writing Creative Nonfiction: Fiction Techniques for Crafting Great Nonfiction*. Berkeley, CA: Ten Speed Press, 2001.

"Conceptual Overview, McGuffey Birthplace & School, Homes Programs." Unpublished manuscript, 29 January 2003. Braden Papers.

Credle, Jamie. "Endless Possibilities: Historic House Museum Programs That Make Educators Sing." In *Interpreting Historic House Museums*, edited by Jessica Foy Donnelly, 269–92. Lanham, MD: AltaMira Press, a Division of Rowman & Littlefield, 2002.

Crew, Spencer R. "Locating Authenticity: Fragments of a Dialogue." In *Exhibiting Cultures: The Poetics and Politics of Museum Display*, edited by Ivan Karp and Steven D. Lavine, 159–75. Washington, DC: Smithsonian Institution Press, 1991.

Cron, Lisa. *Wired for Story: The Writer's Guide to Using Brain Science to Hook Readers from the Very First Sentence*. Berkeley, CA: Ten Speed Press, 2012.

Csikszentmihalyi, Mihaly, and Kim Hermann. "Intrinsic Motivation in Museums: What Makes Visitors Want to Learn?" *Museum News* 74, no. 3 (May/June 1994): 35–37+.

———. "Intrinsic Motivation in Museums: Why Does One Want to Learn?" In *Public Institutions for Personal Learning: Establishing a Research Agenda*, edited by John Falk and Lynne D. Dierking, 66–77. Washington, DC: AAM Technical Information Service, 1995.

Curling, Marianna. "How to Write a Furnishing Plan." *History News* 57, no. 2 (Spring 2002): Technical Leaflet #218.

Deetz, James. "The Changing Historical House Museum: Can It Live?" In *A Living History Reader*, Vol. 1, *Museums*, edited by Jay Anderson, 15–17. Nashville, TN: American Association for State and Local History, 1991.

———. *In Small Things Forgotten: An Archaeology of Early American Life*. Rev. ed. New York: Anchor Books, a Division of Bantam Doubleday Dell Publishing Group, 1996.

————. "The Link from Object to Person to Concept." In *A Living History Reader*. Vol. 1, *Museums*, edited by Jay Anderson, 206–12. Nashville, TN: American Association for State and Local History, 1991.

————. "The Reality of the Pilgrim Fathers." In *A Living History Reader*. Vol. 1, *Museums*, edited by Jay Anderson, 101–109. Nashville, TN: American Association for State and Local History, 1991.

————. "A Sense of Another World: History Museums and Cultural Change." *Museum News* 58, no. 5 (May–June 1980): 40–45.

Dierking, Lynn D., Jessica J. Luke, Kathryn A. Foat, and Leslie Adelman. "The Family and Free-Choice Learning." *Museum News* 80, no. 6 (November/December 2001): 38–43+.

Dierking, Lynn D., Robert Kihne, Ann Grimes Rand, and Marilyn Solvay. "Laughing and Learning Together: Family Learning Research Becomes Practice at the U.S.S. Constitution Museum." *History News* 61, no. 3 (Summer 2006): 12–15.

Disney Institute. *Be Our Guest: Perfecting the Art of Customer Service*. New York: Disney Editions, 2001.

*The Docent Handbook*. Berkeley, CA: National Docent Symposium Council, 2001.

Ellis, Rex M. "The Historic House Furnishings Plan: Process and Product." In *Interpreting Historic House Museums*, edited by Jessica Foy Donnelly, 61–80. Lanham, MD: AltaMira Press, a Division of Rowman & Littlefield, 2002.

Falk, John H., and Lynn D. Dierking. *Learning from Museums: Visitor Experience and the Making of Meaning*. Walnut Creek, CA: Altamira Press, 2000.

————. *Lessons without Limit: How Free-Choice Learning Is Transforming Education*. Walnut Creek, CA: AltaMira Press, 2002.

————. *The Museum Experience*. Washington, DC: Whalesback Books, 1992.

Fischer, Daryl K. "Connecting with Visitor Panels." *Museum News* 76, no. 3 (May/June 1997): 33–37.

Fleming, E. McClung. "Artifact Study: A Proposed Model." *Winterthur Portfolio* 9, no. 4 (1974): 153–73.

Freas, Daniel J., Jennifer L. Ford, and David. R. Scofield. "Chinking Between the Logs: Reinterpreting the Miller House at Meadowcroft Museum of Rural Life." *Proceedings of the 1997 Conference and Annual Meeting*, Staunton, Virginia, edited by Debra A. Reid. Vol. XX (North Bloomfield, OH: The Association for Living Historical Farms and Agricultural Museums, 1998), 200–205.

"General Store Interpretive Program Scripted Role-Playing Presentation." Attachment to email from Jeanine Head Miller to Ann Eskridge. Unpublished manuscript, 6 July 1993. Braden Papers.

"General Store Project, Historic Structure Report, Report #1." Unpublished manuscript, 7 September 1991. Braden Papers.

"General Store Project Plan." Unpublished manuscript, 9 September 1991. Braden Papers.

"General Store Project Proposal Restatement/Program Brief." Unpublished manuscript, 29 May 1992. Braden Papers.

"General Store Reinstallation Project, Review of Assumptions." Unpublished manuscript, 23 January 1992. Braden Papers.

George, Alberta Sebolt. "Keynote Address: Managing for the Future." *Proceedings of the 1990 Annual Meeting, Providence, Rhode Island*, edited by Debra Reid and Ken Yellis. Vol. XIII (Santa Fe, NM: The Association for Living Historical Farms and Agricultural Museums, 1993), 24–33.

Gilbert, Hallie. "Immersive Exhibitions: What's the Big Deal?" *Visitor Studies Today!* 5, no. 111 (Fall 2002): 10–13.

Glines, Timothy, and David Grabitske. "Telling the Story: Better Interpretation at Small Historical Organizations." *History News* 58, no. 2 (Spring 2003): Technical Leaflet #222.

Goldstein, E. Bruce. *Cognitive Psychology: Connecting Mind, Research, and Everyday Experience*, 2nd ed. Belmont, CA: Thomson Higher Education, 2008.

Graburn, Nelson. "The Museum and the Visitor Experience." In *Museum Education Anthology: Perspectives on Informal Learning a Decade of Roundtable Reports, 1973–83*, edited by Susan K. Nichols, Mary Alexander, and Ken Yellis, 177–82. Washington, DC: Museum Education Roundtable, 1984.

Grattan, Virginia L. *Mary Colter: Builder Upon the Red Earth*. Flagstaff, AZ: Northland Press, 1980.

Greene, Katherine, and Richard Greene. *Inside the Dream: The Personal Story of Walt Disney*. New York: Disney Editions, 2001.

Grinder, Alison L., and E. Sue McCoy. *The Good Guide: A Sourcebook for Interpreters, Docents, and Tour Guides.* Scottsdale, AZ: Ironwood Press, 1985.

Gross, Michael P., and Ron Zimmerman. "Park and Museum Interpretation: Helping Visitors Find Meaning." *Curator: The Museum Journal* 45, no. 4 (October 2002): 265–76.

"Grant Proposal, National Endowment for the Humanities. *Your Place in Time: 20th Century America* Exhibition." Unpublished manuscript, 1 February 1999. Braden Papers.

"A Guide to Our Place and Credits (Back to the Land Flipbook text)." Unpublished manuscript, 1999. Braden Papers.

Hague, Stephen. "How to Plan and Implement Interpretation." *History News* 68, no. 2 (Spring 2013): Technical Leaflet #262.

Ham, Sam H. *Environmental Interpretation: A Practical Guide for People with Big Ideas and Small Budgets.* Golden, CO: Fulcrum Publishing, 1993.

———. *Interpretation: Making a Difference on Purpose*. Golden, CO: Fulcrum Publishing, 2013.

"Handout to presenters at J. R. Jones General Store Training Refresh." Unpublished manuscript, 6 April 2015. Braden Papers.

Hartley, Michele. "Shifting the Conversation: Improving Access with Universal Design." *N.A.M.E. Exhibitionist* 34, no. 2 (Fall 2015): 42.

Hawes, Edward L. "The Living History Farm in North America: New Directions in Research and Interpretation." In *A Living History Reader*. Vol. 1, *Museums*, edited by Jay Anderson, 79–97. Nashville, TN: American Association for State and Local History, 1991.

———. "Planning Living History Programs and Facilities: Seven Areas of Concern." *Proceedings of the Annual Meetings Held at Ottawa, Santa Fe, and Old Salem*

*1978-1980*, edited by Virginia Briscoe (Washington, DC: The Association for Living Historical Farms and Agricultural Museums, 1981), 22–27.

Hench, John, with Peggy Van Pelt. *Designing Disney: Imagineering and the Art of the Show*. New York: Disney Editions, 2003.

Herbst, John, and Trina Nelson Thomas. "The Power of Personal Connections." *History News* 67, no. 2 (Spring 2012): 17–20.

Herrman, Douglas, and Dana Plude, "Museum Memory." In *Public Institutions for Personal Learning: Establishing a Research Agenda*, edited by John Falk and Lynne D. Dierking, 53–66. Washington, DC: AAM Technical Information Service, 1995.

Hindle, Brooke, "How Much Is a Piece of the True Cross Worth?" In *Material Culture and the Study of American Life: A Winterthur Book*, edited by Ian M. G. Quimby, 5–20. New York: W.W. Norton, 1978.

"History of the General Store Building/Getting the History Right." Unpublished manuscript, n.d., ca. 1993. Braden Papers.

Howe, Barbara J., Dolores A. Fleming, Emory L. Kemp, and Ruth Ann Overbeck. *Houses and Homes: Exploring Their History*, The Nearby History Series, vol. 2. Nashville, TN: American Association for State and Local History, 1987.

Hughes, Catherine. *Museum Theatre: Communicating with Visitors through Drama*. Portsmouth, NH: Heinemann, 1998.

The Imagineers. *Walt Disney Imagineering: A Behind the Dreams Look at Making the Magic Real*. New York: Hyperion, 1996.

Institute for Learning Innovation. "'America on the Move' Exhibition, Front-End Study, Best Practice Analysis." Unpublished manuscript, September 2000.

Ivcevic, Zorana, Nadine Maliakkal, and the Botin Foundation. "Teaching Emotion and Creativity Skills through the Arts." In *Fostering Empathy through Museums*, edited by Elif M. Gokcigdem, 1–19. Lanham, MD: Rowman & Littlefield, 2016.

Johnson, Mary. "What's in a Butterchurn or a Sadiron? Some Thoughts on Using Artifacts in Social History." *The Public Historian* 5, no 1 (Winter 1983): 60–81.

Jones, Dale. "Living History in the City." *History News* 50, no. 3 (Summer 1995): 10–13.

———. "Personal Connections and the Great Cosmic Soup." *History News* 63, no. 2 (Spring 2008): 14–18.

———. "Theater 101 for Historical Interpretation." *History News* 59, no. 3 (Summer 2004): Technical Leaflet #227.

"The J. R. Jones General Store in Greenfield Village, Program Plan, Donna R. Braden and Blake D. Hayes." Unpublished manuscript, 15 September 1992. Braden Papers.

"J. R. Jones General Store Presenter Manual." Unpublished manuscript, 2018. Braden Papers.

"J. R. Jones General Store Presenter Training Manual." Unpublished manuscript, April 1994. Braden Papers.

"J. R. Jones General Store Training Manual." Unpublished manuscript, March 2017. Braden Papers.

Kahn, Lloyd, and Bob Easton. *Shelter*. Bolinas, CA: Shelter Publications, Inc., 1973.

Kaplan, Stephen, Lisa V. Bardwell, and Deborah B. Slakter. "The Museum as a Restorative Environment." *Environment and Behavior* 25 (1993): 725–42. http://eab.sagepub.com/cgi/content/abstract/25/6/725.

Katz-Hyman, Martha B., and Mick Woodcock. "The Basics of Writing Furnishings Plans." *Proceedings of the 2000 Conference and Annual Meeting*, Mystic, Connecticut, edited by Ron Kley and Jane Radcliffe. Vol. XXIII (North Bloomfield, OH: The Association for Living History, Farm and Agricultural Museums, 2001), 158–62.

Kelleher, Tom. "Old Sturbridge Village: From Re-Created Historic Village to History Learning 'Center.'" *Proceedings of the 2005 Conference and Annual Meeting, Living History Farms, Des Moines, Iowa,* edited by Debra A. Reid and Carol E. Kennis. Vol. XXVIII (North Bloomfield, OH: The Association for Living History, Farm and Agricultural Museums, 2005), 12–17.

Kelsey, Darwin. "Harvests of History." In *A Living History Reader.* Vol. 1, *Museums,* edited by Jay Anderson, 69–72. Nashville, TN: American Association for State and Local History, 1991.

Kilsdonk, Betty. "Is Process Demonstration Historically Credible?" *Proceedings of the 1987 Annual Meeting, Ann Arbor and Dearborn, Michigan, The Association for Living Historical Farms and Agricultural Museums*, edited by Peter Cousins. Vol. X (Washington, DC: Smithsonian Institution, 1989), 20–32.

Klingler, Stacy, and Conny Graft. "In Lieu of Mind Reading: Visitor Studies and Evaluation." In *The Small Museum Toolkit.* Book 4, *Reaching and Responding to the Audience*, edited by Cinnamon Catlin-Legutko and Stacy Klingler, 37–74. Lanham, MD: AltaMira Press, a Division of Rowman & Littlefield, 2012.

Korn, Randi. "Studying Your Visitors: Where to Begin." In *Introduction to Museum Evaluation*, edited by Minda Borun and Randi Korn, 5–9. Washington, DC: American Association of Museums, 1999.

Kyvig, David E., and Myron A. Marty. *Nearby History: Exploring the Past Around You.* 3rd ed. Lanham, MD: Rowman & Littlefield, 2010.

Larsen, Judith. "To Label or Not? Visitors Win: New Life for an Immersion Exhibit." *Visitor Studies Today!* (Summer 2002): 11–16.

Latham, Kiersten. "Numinous Experiences with Museum Objects." *Visitor Studies* 16, no. 1 (2013): 3–20.

———. "The Poetry of the Museum: A Holistic Model of Numinous Museum Experiences." *Museum Management and Curatorship* 22, no. 3 (September 2007): 247–63.

Latham, Kiersten, and Elizabeth Wood. *The Objects of Experience: Transforming Visitor-Object Encounters in Museums.* Walnut Creek, CA: Left Coast Press, Inc., 2014.

Leffler, Phyllis K., and Joseph Brent. *Public History Readings, Application II: Secondary Sources.* Malabar, FL: Krieger Publishing Co., 1992.

Leon, Warren, and Margaret Piatt. "Living-History Museums." In *History Museums in the United States: A Critical Assessment*, edited by Warren Leon and Roy Rosenzweig, 64–97. Urbana: University of Illinois Press, 1989.

Levy, Barbara Abramoff. "Historic House Tours that Succeed: Choosing the Best Tour Approach." In *Interpreting Historic House Museums*, edited by Jessica Foy

Donnelly, 192–209. Walnut Creek, CA: AltaMira Press, a Division of Rowman & Littlefield, 2002.

———. "Interpretation Planning: Why and How." In *Interpreting Historic House Museums*, edited by Jessica Foy Donnelly, 43–60. Lanham, MD: AltaMira Press, a Division of Rowman & Littlefield, 2002.

Levy, Barbara Abramoff, Sandra McKenzie Lloyd, and Susan Porter Schreiber. *Great Tours! Thematic Tours and Guide Training for Historic Sites.* Walnut Creek, CA: AltaMira, a Division of Rowman & Littlefield, 2001.

Lloyd, Sandra Mackenzie. "Creating Memorable Visits: How to Develop and Implement Theme-Based Tours." In *Interpreting Historic House Museums*, edited by Jessica Foy Donnelly, 210–30. Walnut Creek, CA: AltaMira Press, a Division of Rowman & Littlefield, 2002.

Lowenthal, David. *The Past Is a Foreign Country.* Cambridge: Cambridge University Press, 1985.

———. "The Timeless Past: Some Anglo-American Historical Preconceptions." In *Memory and American History*, edited by David Thelen, 134–51. Bloomington: Indiana University Press, 1990.

Lyon, Cherstin M., Elizabeth M. Nix, and Rebecca K. Shrum. *Introduction to Public History: Interpreting the Past, Engaging Audiences.* Lanham, MD: Rowman & Littlefield, 2007.

Malmberg, Melody. *The Making of Disney's Animal Kingdom Theme Park.* New York: Hyperion, 1998.

Marling, Karal Ann. *As Seen on TV: The Visual Culture of Everyday Life in the 1950s.* Cambridge, MA: Harvard University Press, 1994.

———. "Imagineering the Disney Theme Parks." In *Designing Disney's Theme Parks: The Architecture of Reassurance*, edited by Karal Ann Marling, 29–177. Paris: Flammarion, 1997.

Marling, Karal Ann, with Donna R. Braden. *Behind the Magic: 50 Years of Disneyland.* Dearborn, MI: The Henry Ford, 2005.

"McGuffey Birthplace Audio Script." Attachment to email from Jeanine Head Miller to Donna Braden and Cathy Cwiek. Unpublished manuscript, 11 April 2003. Braden Papers.

"McGuffey Birthplace Furnishing Plan." Unpublished manuscripts, 10 April 2003; 29 April 2003; 5 May 2003. Braden Papers.

"McGuffey Birthplace Program Proposal." Unpublished manuscript, July 1998. Braden Papers.

"The McGuffey Birthplace: Updated Information for a Proposed New Program." Unpublished manuscript, 15 June 1998. Braden Papers.

"McGuffey Web Component." Unpublished manuscript, 2003. Braden Papers.

McKenna-Cress, Polly, and Janet Kamien. *Creating Exhibitions: Collaboration in the Planning, Development, and Design of Innovative Experiences.* Hoboken, NJ: John Wiley and Sons, 2013.

McLean, Kathleen. *Planning for People in Museum Exhibitions.* Washington, DC: The Association of Science-Technology Centers, 1993.

McRainey, D. Lynn. "A Sense of the Past." In *Connecting Kids to History with Museum Exhibitions*, edited by D. Lynn McRainey and John Russick, 155–72. Walnut Creek, CA: Left Coast Press, 2010.

Meisinger, Leona. "Using Primary Sources to Enhance Living History Programming." *Proceedings of the 1997 Conference and Annual Meeting, Staunton, Virginia*, edited by Debra A. Reid. Vol. XX (North Bloomfield, OH: The Association for Living Historical Farms and Agricultural Museums, 1998), 209–11.

Montell, Lynwood. "Social History and Today's Museum." *Proceedings of the Annual Meeting April 6–9, 1981, Golden Pond and Lake Barkley, Kentucky, The Association for Living Historical Farms and Agricultural Museums* (Washington, DC: Smithsonian Institution, 1983), 6–13.

Mouw, Michael, and Daniel Spock. "Immersive Media: Creating Theatrical Storytelling Experiences." In *The Digital Museum: A Think Guide*, edited by Herminia Din and Phyllis Hecht, 45–56. Washington, DC: American Association of Museums, 2007.

National Association for Museum Exhibition. "Creating an Inclusive Experience: Exhibitions and Universal Design." *N.A.M.E. Exhibitionist* (entire issue) 34, no. 2 (Fall 2015).

———. "Enriching the Visitor Experience for Kids and Families." *N.A.M.E. Exhibitionist* (entire issue) 27, no. 1 (Spring 2008).

———. "Meaning-Making in Museums," *N.A.M.E. Exhibitionist* (entire issue) 18, no. 2 (Fall 1999).

———. "Meaning-Making Revisited." *N.A.M.E. Exhibitionist* (entire issue) 32, no. 3 (Spring 2013).

National Park Service Harpers Ferry Center. "Guidelines for Preparing Historic Furnishings Reports." Accessed March, 21, 2018. https://www.nps.gov/hfc/products/furnish/furnish-plan-hfr-guide.cfm.

Nilsen, Adam P., and Mariam Bader. "The Psychology of Empathy: Compelling Possibilities for Museums." In *Fostering Empathy through Museums*, edited by Elif M. Gokcigdem, 115–27. Lanham, MD: Rowman & Littlefield, 2016.

Packer, Jan. "Beyond Learning: Exploring Visitors' Perceptions of the Value and Benefits of Museum Experiences." *Curator* 51, no. 1 (January 2008): 33–54.

Parman, Alice, Ann Craig, Lyle Murphy, Liz White, and Lauren Willis. *Exhibit Makeovers: A Do-It Yourself Workbook for Small Museums*. 2nd ed. Lanham, MD: Rowman & Littlefield/AASLH, 2017.

Piatt, Margaret. "Engaging Visitors through Effective Communication." In *Interpreting Historic House Museums*, edited by Jessica Foy Donnelly, 231–50. Walnut Creek, CA: AltaMira Press, a Division of Rowman & Littlefield, 2002.

"Preliminary Historic Structure Report, William Holmes McGuffey Birthplace." Unpublished manuscript, 13 September 1989. Braden Papers.

Prown, Jules David. "Mind in Matter: An Introduction to Material Culture Theory and Method." *Winterthur Portfolio* 17, no. 1 (Spring 1982): 1–19.

Rand, Judy. "Less Is More. And More Is Less." *Exhibition: A Journal of Exhibition Theory & Practice for Museum Professionals* 32, no. 1 (Spring 2016): 36–41. Accessed June 23, 2018. https://static1.squarespace.com/static/58fa260a725e25c4f30020f3/t/594d16c51b631be4c390c593/1498224358446/11_Exhibition_LessIsMore.pdf.

————. "Write and Design with the Family in Mind." In *Connecting Kids to History with Museum Exhibitions*, edited by D. Lynn McRainey and John Russick, 257–84. Walnut Creek, CA: Left Coast Press, Inc., 2010.

Rand, Judy, Ann Grimes, Robert Kihne, and Sarah Watkins. "Families First! Rethinking Exhibits to Engage All Ages." *History News* 64, no. 1 (Winter 2009): Technical Leaflet #245.

Raphling, Britt, and Beverley Serrell. "Capturing Affective Learning." *Current Trends in Audience Research and Evaluation.* Vol. 7 (Washington, DC: American Association of Museums Committee on Audience Research and Evaluation, 1993), 57–64.

"The Reason Why We're Here." [Notes for Back-to-the-Land Commune backstory]. Unpublished manuscript, n.d., ca. 1999. Braden Papers.

Ritchie, Donald A. *Doing Oral History: A Practical Guide.* 3rd ed. New York: Oxford University Press, 2015.

Roberts, Lisa. "The Elusive Quality of 'Affect.'" In *What Research Says about Learning in Science Museums*, edited by Beverly Serrell, 19–22. Washington, DC: Association of Science-Technology Centers, 1990.

Rodley, Ed. "Tilting at Windmills, Part One." *Thinking about Museums* (blog). October 29, 2013. http://exhibitdev.wordpress.com/2013/10/29/tilting-at-windmills -part-one/.

Rohde, Joe M. "Creating Narrative Space." *ICAM* 15, Paris Session 4 (May 2, 2010): 4. http://www.icam-web.org/data/media/cms_binary/original/1284051324.pdf.

————. "From Myth to Mountain: Insights into Virtual Placemaking." *ACM Siggraph Computer Graphics Newsletter, Article No. 1* 41, no. 3 (August 2007). https:// dl.acm.org/citation.cfm?id=1281325&dl=ACM&coll=DL&CFID=1018184222& CFTOKEN=72395515.

Rosenzweig, Roy, and David Thelen. *The Presence of the Past: Popular Uses of History in American Life.* New York: Columbia University Press, 1998.

Roth, Stacy F. *Past into Present: Effective Techniques for First-Person Historical Interpretation.* Chapel Hill: University of North Carolina Press, 1998.

Schlereth, Thomas J., ed. *Material Culture Studies in America.* Lanham, MD: AltaMira Press, a Division of Rowman & Littlefield, 1999.

Science Leaning, Inc. "'Points in Time' exhibition, Summative Evaluation." Heinz History Center, Pittsburgh, PA. Unpublished manuscript, 1997.

Scientific American. "What Brain Activity Can Explain Suspension of Disbelief?" January 1, 2014. https://www.scientificamerican.com/article/what-brain-activity -can-explain-sus/.

Screven, Chandler G. "Motivating Visitors to Read Labels." In *Text in the Exhibition Medium*, edited by Andrée Blais, 97–132. Quebec City: La Société des Musées Québécois and Musée de la Civilisation, 1994.

Seale, William. *Recreating the Historic House Interior.* Nashville, TN: American Association for State and Local History, 1979.

Serrell, Beverly. *Exhibit Labels: An Interpretive Approach.* 2nd ed. Lanham, MD: Rowman & Littlefield, 2015.

Shaffer, Sharon. "Never Too Young to Connect to History: Cognitive Development and Learning." In *Connecting Kids to History with Museum Exhibitions*, edited by D. Lynn McRainey and John Russick, 31–47. Walnut Creek, CA: Left Coast Press, 2010.

Silverman, Lois. "Making Meaning Together: Lessons from the Field of American History." *Journal of Museum Education* 18, no. 3 (Fall 1993): 7–11.

———. "Taking a Wider View of Museum Outcomes and Experiences: Theory, Research, and Magic." Madeleine Mainstone Lecture, *Journal of Education in Museums* 23 (2002): 3–8.

———. "Visitor Meaning-Making in Museums for a New Age." *Curator* 38, no. 3 (1995): 161–70.

Spock, Daniel. 2008. "A Practical Guide to Personal Connectivity." *History News* 63, no. 4 (Autumn 2008): 11–17.

———. "Imagination: A Child's Gateway to Engagement with the Past." In *Connecting Kids to History with Museum Exhibitions*, edited by D. Lynn McRainey and John Russick, 117–35. Walnut Creek, CA: Left Coast Press, 2010.

Stanford Encyclopedia of Philosophy. "Mental Imagery." November 18, 1997 with substantive revision September 12, 2014. https://plato.stanford.edu/entries/mental-imagery/index.html.

Stearns, Peter N. "The New Social History: An Overview." In *Ordinary People and Everyday Life: Perspectives on New Social History*, edited by James B. Gardner and George Rollie Adams, 3–21. Nashville, TN: American Association for State and Local History, 1983.

Stein, Jill, Marianna Adams, and Jessica Luke. "Thinking Evaluatively: A Practical Guide to Integrating the Visitor Voice." *History News* 62, no. 2 (Spring 2007): Technical Leaflet #238.

Sugawara, Bethany Watkins. "But They're Not Real! Rethinking the Use of Props in Historic House Museum Displays." *History News* 58, no. 4 (August 2003): 20–23.

"Summative Evaluation. *Your Place in Time: 20th Century America* exhibition." Unpublished manuscript, 2001. Braden Papers.

Summers, John. *Creating Exhibits That Engage: A Manual for Museums and Historical Organizations*. Lanham, MD: Rowman & Littlefield/AASLH, 2018.

Sweeney, John A. H. "Introduction." In *Material Culture and the Study of American Life: A Winterthur Book*, edited by Ian M. G. Quimby, 1–4. New York: W.W. Norton, 1978.

Tari, Emilie. "Old World Wisconsin: What Price Our Heritage?" *Wisconsin Academy Review* 30, no. 2 (March 1984): 47–52.

Taylor, Sam, and Beverly Serrell, eds. *Try It! Improving Exhibits through Formative Evaluation*. Washington, DC: Association of Science-Technology Centers, 1992.

Thomas, Bob. *Walt Disney: An American Original*. New York: Walt Disney Company, 1976.

Tilden, Freeman. *Interpreting Our Heritage*. 2nd ed. Chapel Hill: University of North Carolina Press, 1967.

Tramposch, William. "Mickey and the Muses." *History News* 53, no. 1 (Winter 1998): 10–16.

Vanderstel, David G. "A Behavioral Approach to Living History: The Search for Community in the Past." *Proceedings of the Annual Meetings in Denver, Colorado, and Williamsburg, Virginia, The Association for Living Historical Farms and Agricultural Museums*, edited by Donna R. Braden. Vol. VIII (Washington, DC: Smithsonian Institution, 1988), 76–87.

Veverka, John A. *Interpretive Master Planning.* Vol. 1, *Strategies for the New Millennium.* Edinburgh: MuseumsEtc, 2011.

———. *Interpretive Master Planning.* Vol. 2, *Selected Essays: Philosophy, Theory, Practice.* Edinburgh: MuseumsEtc, 2011.

Walhimer, Mark. "Museum Exhibition Design, Part VI. Exhibition Evaluation" (blog). Museum Planner website. July 10, 2012. https://museumplanner.org/museum-exhibition-design-part-vi/.

Wallace, Mike. *Mickey Mouse History and Other Essays on American Memory.* Philadelphia, PA: Temple University Press, 1996.

Warner, Mary. "House History: Some Assembly Required." *History News* 64, no. 3 (Summer 2009): Technical Leaflet #247.

Wenzel, Dorothy. "Using Primary Sources to Recreate a Living History Site." *Proceedings of the 1997 Conference and Annual Meeting, Staunton, Virginia*, edited by Debra A. Reid. Vol. XX (North Bloomfield, OH: The Association for Living Historical Farms and Agricultural Museums, 1998), 206–208.

Wilkening, Susie, and Erica Donnis. "Authenticity? It Means Everything." *History News* 63, no. 4 (Autumn 2008): 18–23.

Wilkening, Susie, and James Chung. *Life Stages of the Museum Visitor: Building Engagement over a Lifetime.* Washington, DC: The AAM Press, 2009.

"William Holmes McGuffey Historic Presenter Training Manual," Donna R. Braden, Cathy Cwiek, Jeanine Head Miller. Unpublished manuscript, 2003. Braden Papers.

Woodcock, Mick. "Physical Control for Collections: Keeping It on the Table after Bringing It All to the Table." *Proceedings of the 2013 Conference and Annual Meeting, Hale Farm & Village, Akron, Ohio*, edited by Debra A. Reid. Vol. XXXVI (North Bloomfield, OH: The Association for Living History, Farm and Agricultural Museums, 2014), 105–107.

Yellis, Ken. "Not Time Machines, But Real Time: Living History at Plimoth Plantation." *Proceedings of the 1989 Annual Meeting, Indianapolis, Indiana, The Association for Living Historical Farms and Agricultural Museums*, edited by Thomas A. Woods. Vol. XII (Santa Fe, NM: Old Cienega Village Museum, 1992), 52–57.

# Index

Page references for figures are italicized.

# About the Author

**Donna R. Braden**, senior curator and curator of public life at The Henry Ford in Dearborn, Michigan, has spent more than four decades in the museum field. Both at The Henry Ford and as an independent consultant, her career has cut across numerous aspects of museum practice, including material culture expertise, collections development and analysis, historical research, interpretive planning, exhibition development, and visitor studies. Her creation of rigorously researched, story-based environments in both museum exhibitions and historic structures stands out as a benchmark of the integration between these disciplines.

Braden has published widely and presented at numerous conferences on topics ranging from the exhibition process to creating dynamic interpretive manuals to what museums can learn from Walt Disney. She is a past president of ALHFAM (Association for Living History, Farm and Agricultural Museums) and a recipient of the John T. Schlebecker Award for her contributions to the field of living history. She received her bachelor's degree in Anthropology from Ohio State University, with distinction in American Cultural History, and obtained a master's degree from the Winterthur Program in Early American Culture, with a certificate in Museum Studies, from the University of Delaware. In 2013, she obtained a second master's degree, in Liberal Studies, from the University of Michigan-Dearborn.